PAWNEE MUSIC

Da Capo Press Music Reprint Series

PAWNEE MUSIC

By Frances Densmore

DA CAPO PRESS · NEW YORK · 1972

Library of Congress Cataloging in Publication Data

Densmore, Frances, 1867-1957.
  Pawnee music.

  (Da Capo Press music reprint series)
  Reprint of the 1929 ed., which was issued as Bulletin
93 of Smithsonian Institution. Bureau of American
Ethnology.
  Bibliography: p.
  1. Indians of North America—Music. 2. Pawnee
Indians. I. Title. II. Series: U.S. Bureau of
American Ethnology. Bulletin 93.
ML3557.D368   1972   784.7'51   72-1880
ISBN 0-306-70508-7

This Da Capo Press edition of *Pawnee Music* is an
unabridged republication of the first edition
published in Washington, D.C., in 1929 as Bulletin
93 of the Bureau of American Ethnology, Smithsonian
Institution.

Published by Da Capo Press, Inc.
A Subsidiary of Plenum Publishing Corporation
227 West 17th Street, New York, New York 10011

PAWNEE MUSIC

SMITHSONIAN INSTITUTION
BUREAU OF AMERICAN ETHNOLOGY
BULLETIN 93

PAWNEE MUSIC

BY

FRANCES DENSMORE

UNITED STATES
GOVERNMENT PRINTING OFFICE
WASHINGTON : 1929

LETTER OF TRANSMITTAL

SMITHSONIAN INSTITUTION,
BUREAU OF AMERICAN ETHNOLOGY,
Washington, D. C., April 16, 1929.

SIR: I have the honor to transmit the accompanying manuscript, entitled "Pawnee Music," by Miss Frances Densmore, and to recommend its publication as a bulletin of the Bureau of American Ethnology.

Very respectfully yours,

M. W. STIRLING,
Chief.

DR. CHARLES G. ABBOT,
Secretary of the Smithsonian Institution.

FOREWORD

The previous studies of Indian music [1] have included no tribe in which ceremonialism is so highly developed as among the Pawnee, whose songs are here presented. This research was conducted among members of the Skidi and Chaui Bands near Pawnee, Okla., in 1919 and 1920. Portions of two important ceremonies were witnessed and several gatherings of a ceremonial character were attended during the progress of the work. The ceremonies were those of the Morning Star and the Painting of the Buffalo Skull, the writer being admitted to the Morning Star lodge during the former ceremony and witnessing the Buffalo and Lance dances, which are a part of the latter. The gatherings included hand games, and dances in honor of Pawnee soldiers upon their return from the recent war.

Grateful acknowledgment is made of assistance rendered by interpreters, especially by Mr. James R. Murie, chief of the Skidi Band, who explained many tribal customs and who wrote down and interpreted the words of the songs. The writer also acknowledges the courtesy of Dr. John R. Swanton in standardizing the orthography of the Pawnee words.

---

[1] Chippewa Music, Bull. 45; Chippewa Music II, Bull. 53; Teton Sioux Music, Bull. 61; Northern Ute Music, Bull. 75; Mandan and Hidatsa Music, Bull. 80; Papago Music, Bull. 90, Bur. Amer. Ethn.; and Music of the Tule Indians of Panama, Smithsonian Misc. Colls., vol. 77, no. 11.

CONTENTS

ILLUSTRATIONS

LIST OF SONGS

1. Arranged in Order of Serial Numbers

Songs Connected with Folk Tales

Unclassified Songs

2. Arranged in Order of Catalogue Numbers

Catalogue No.	Title of song	Name of singer	Serial No.	Page
1077	The little rattlesnake	Mrs. Blain	77	108
1078	"Old age is painful"	----do	23	50
1079	"You need not fear the horse"	----do	78	109
1080	"Our hearts are set in the heavens"	----do	64	90
1081	Lance dance song (a)	----do	27	55
1082	Women's war song	----do	38	68
1083	Raven Lance Society song	----do	25	53
1084	Song concerning Mother Moon	----do	51	80
1085	Brown Bear's song	----do	37	68
1086	"The thunder spoke quietly"	----do	33	61
1087	"The crow"	----do	50	79
1088	Running Scout's Ghost dance song	----do	58	85
1089	"My trust is in Mother Corn"	----do	67	93
1090	"It is good where we are now"	----do	66	92
1091	"The band of the dead is coming"	----do	10	36
1092	"Father gave me a pipe"	----do	85	115
1093	Lance dance song (b)	----do	28	56
1094	Song concerning an open grave	----do	52	81
1095	"You came near finding them"	----do	49	78
1096	Mad Chief mourns for his grandson	----do	86	119
1097	Hand game song concerning a little boy.	----do	48	77
1098	"I hear the sound of a child crying"	----do	47	76
1099	Mother's song for a dead baby	----do	83	113
1100	Song of a warrior's wife	----do	70	96
1101	"Other girls are as pretty as she"	----do	71	97
1102	Song concerning the Ghost dance	Mr. Blain	59	86
1103	"The white fox"	----do	29	57

2. Arranged in Order of Catalogue Numbers—Continued

Catalogue No.	Title of song	Name of singer	Serial No.	Page
1104	"A woman welcomes the warriors"	Mr. Blain	35	64
1105	Song to comfort a child's grief	do	82	113
1106	"It is mine, this country wide"	do	30	58
1107	"The yellow star"	do	57	84
1108	Song concerning Iron Shirt	do	31	60
1109	"Yonder the smoke was standing"	do	5	30
1110	"The woman imitates the buffalo"	do	6	31
1111	"Unreal the buffalo is standing"	do	9	35
1112	"My dear father the buffalo"	do	4	28
1113	"The waves of dust"	do	8	33
1114	"The herd passes through the village"	do	2	25
1115	"The buffalo are coming"	do	7	32
1116	"The buffalo and the crow"	do	3	27
1117	"Mother is coming"	do	11	37
1118	"A woman stands among the trees"	do	13	40
1119	"The bear is pointing at the sun"	do	12	38
1120	"The horse is shouting"	do	14	41
1121	"I was lost in the timber"	do	15	42
1122	"The heavens are speaking"	John Luwak	61	88
1123	"I am exalted among the people"	do	60	87
1124	"The Lance dancers"	do	26	54
1125	"He comes"	do	34	63
1126	"The message of a star"	do	81	112
1127	A poor man's prayer	do	79	110
1128	Eagle Chief's war song	do	32	61
1129	"O expanse of the heavens"	do	62	89
1130	"Power is in the heavens"	do	63	90
1131	Man Chief's song	do	65	91
1132	Song received from a dead relative	do	84	114
1133	"Beloved emblem"	do	24	52
1134	Song for returned Pawnee soldiers	do	36	66
1135	Song of affection (b)	do	69	95
1136	Song of affection (a)	do	68	94
1137	Blue Hawk's hand game song	Horse Chief	39	71
1138	Hand game guessing song (a)	do	40	71
1139	Hand game guessing song (b)	do	41	72
1140	Hand game guessing song (c)	do	42	73
1141	Hand game guessing song (d)	do	43	73
1142	Hand game guessing song (e)	do	44	74
1143	Hand game guessing song (f)	do	45	75
1144	Hand game guessing song (g)	do	46	75
1145	Ghost dance song (a)	do	53	81
1146	Ghost dance song (b)	do	54	82
1147	Ghost dance song (c)	do	55	82
1148	Ghost dance song (d)	do	56	83
1149	"I am like a bear"	Dog Chief	16	43
1150	Bear dance song (b)	do	18	45
1151	Bear dance song (d)	do	20	47

2. ARRANGED IN ORDER OF CATALOGUE NUMBERS—Continued

Catalogue No.	Title of song	Name of singer	Serial No.	Page
1152	Bear dance song (c)_____	Dog Chief_____	19	46
1153	Bear dance song (a)_____	_____do_____	17	44
1154	Song of Coyote_____	Mrs. Mary Murie	74	103
1155	Song of the strange little boy_____	_____do_____	75	104
1156	Song as the boys flew away_____	_____do_____	76	106
1157	Folk tale song (a) _____	Fannie Chapman__	72	100
1158	Folk tale song (b) _____	_____do_____	73	102
1159	"How near is the morning?"_____	Mark Evarts_____	21	48
1160	"Spring is opening"_____	_____do_____	22	49
1161	"Everything will be right"_____	Mrs. Good Eagle__	80	111
1162	Song of Morning Star_____	Coming Sun_____	1	20

SPECIAL SIGNS USED IN TRANSCRIPTIONS OF SONGS

These signs are intended simply as aids to the student in becoming acquainted with the songs. They should be understood as supplementary to the descriptive analysis rather than a part of the musical notation.

+ placed above a note shows that the tone was sung slightly higher than the indicated pitch. In many instances the tones designated by this and the following sign were "unfocused tones," or were tones whose intonation varied in the several renditions of the song. The intonation of these tones was not such as to suggest the intentional use of "fractional intervals" by the singer.

— placed above a note shows that the tone was sung slightly lower than the indicated pitch.

(. placed above a note shows that the tone was prolonged slightly beyond the indicated time. This and the following sign are used only when the deviation from strict time is less than half the time unit of the song and appears to be unimportant. In many instances the duration of the tones thus marked is variable in the several renditions of the song.

.) placed above a note shows that the tone was given slightly less than the indicated time.

⌐‾‾‾‾‾⌐ placed above a series of notes indicates that these tones constitute a rhythmic unit.

PHONETICS

All consonants have the English sounds except that x represents the palatal spirant.

All vowels have the continental sounds except that å is a obscure.

Âu (diphthong) is pronounced as *ow* in *how*.

NAMES OF SINGERS

Common name	Pawnee name	Translation	Number of songs recorded
Mrs. Wicita Blain (Effie Blain).	Tsastawinahiïgat_ _ _ _	She led a pony into the ceremony.	25
Wicita Blain [1]_ _ _ _ _ _ _ _ _ _	Tutukrawitsu_ _ _ _ _ _ _	He overtook the enemy.	20
John Luwak [2]_ _ _ _ _ _ _ _ _ _	Laduda desadu_ _ _ _ _ _	He does everything as a chief.	15
Horse Chief (Spotted Horse Chief).[3]	_ _ _ _ _ _ _ _ _ _ _ _ _ _ _ _ _ _ _ _	_ _ _ _ _ _ _ _ _ _ _ _ _ _ _ _ _ _ _ _	12
Dog Chief (Simond Adams).	_ _ _ _ _ _ _ _ _ _ _ _ _ _ _ _ _ _ _ _	_ _ _ _ _ _ _ _ _ _ _ _ _ _ _ _ _ _ _ _	5
Mrs. Mary Murie [4]_ _ _ _ _ _	_ _ _ _ _ _ _ _ _ _ _ _ _ _ _ _ _ _ _ _	_ _ _ _ _ _ _ _ _ _ _ _ _ _ _ _ _ _ _ _	3
Fannie Chapman_ _ _ _ _ _ _ _	_ _ _ _ _ _ _ _ _ _ _ _ _ _ _ _ _ _ _ _	_ _ _ _ _ _ _ _ _ _ _ _ _ _ _ _ _ _ _ _	2
Mark Evarts_ _ _ _ _ _ _ _ _ _ _	_ _ _ _ _ _ _ _ _ _ _ _ _ _ _ _ _ _ _ _	_ _ _ _ _ _ _ _ _ _ _ _ _ _ _ _ _ _ _ _	2
Mrs. Good Eagle (Nora White).	_ _ _ _ _ _ _ _ _ _ _ _ _ _ _ _ _ _ _ _	_ _ _ _ _ _ _ _ _ _ _ _ _ _ _ _ _ _ _ _	1
Coming Sun [5]_ _ _ _ _ _ _ _ _ _	_ _ _ _ _ _ _ _ _ _ _ _ _ _ _ _ _ _ _ _	_ _ _ _ _ _ _ _ _ _ _ _ _ _ _ _ _ _ _ _	1
Total_ _ _ _ _ _ _ _ _ _	_ _ _ _ _ _ _ _ _ _ _ _ _ _ _ _ _ _ _ _	_ _ _ _ _ _ _ _ _ _ _ _ _ _ _ _ _ _ _ _	86

[1] Died Dec. 20, 1927.

[2] This singer is commonly known as John Rowak, according to the pronunciation of the Skidi Band. He is a chief of the Chaui Band and requested that his name be presented with the letter *L* used by the Chaui. The words of his songs are presented in the form used by the Skidi in order that they may be uniform with the majority of recorded Pawnee songs.

[3] Died June 13, 1923.

[4] Died June 12, 1928.

[5] Died Nov. 18, 1921.

CHARACTERIZATION OF SINGERS

A majority of these songs were recorded by Wicita Blain and his wife, who are members of the Skidi Band and spent their early years in Nebraska, before the removal of the tribe to Oklahoma. Both were afflicted with blindness and, when recording their songs, were led by a granddaughter who acted as interpreter. Mr. Blain recorded songs of the Lance and Buffalo dances which are his by right of inheritance. In the Buffalo dance attended by the writer he led the songs, being seated back of the "altar"; he also took a prominent part in the Lance dance. Mrs. Effie Blain is considered an equally reliable singer of the old songs.

John Luwak (pl. 2, *a*), who recorded many songs, is chief of the Chaui Band and a fine example of the old-time Indian. He speaks practically no English, but is ambitious to accept the best customs of the white man. In accordance with his request, the phonograph was taken to his home, at some distance from Pawnee, and a majority of his songs were recorded there, with his niece acting as interpreter.

Dog Chief (pl. 1) is one of the oldest members of the tribe and is highly respected.

Horse Chief is one of the younger men and wears his hair in two long, shining braids. He is one of the leading singers at dances.

Mark Evarts (pl. 2, *b*) is a quiet, conservative member of the tribe. Mrs. Good Eagle (pl. 2, *c*) also is held in high esteem.

Mrs. Mary Murie and Fannie Chapman are known as excellent story tellers.

Coming Sun is a prominent member of the Skidi Band. He asked that his English name be withheld because of the importance of certain material which he had contributed to this work.

DOG CHIEF

a, John Luwak

b, Mark Evarts

c, Mrs. Good Eagle

PAWNEE MUSIC

By Frances Densmore

THE PAWNEE TRIBE

The Pawnee is commonly regarded as the last of the Caddoan Tribes which migrated in a general northeasterly direction at an early date.[1] When the Siouan Tribes entered the valley of the Platte River in Nebraska they found the Pawnee already established in that region. The Pawnee called themselves by a term meaning "men of men." Their present name was probably given by some neighboring tribe and derived from *pariki*, meaning a horn, as it was the Pawnee custom to shave the head except a narrow strip extending from the forehead to the scalplock and to stiffen this ridge of hair with grease and paint, curving it upward like a horn.

While in Nebraska the Pawnee lived in earth lodges which were in four permanent groups of villages, each having its geographical location along the Platte River. The people of each group were a unit, representing a division of the tribe. The Skidi (Wolf Pawnee) was in the northwest, its people considering themselves related to the Arikara, another Caddoan Tribe living some distance to the north. The Pitahauerat (Tapage Pawnee) were downstream, the Kithahki (Republican Pawnee) were upstream, and the Chaui (Grand Pawnee) were located between the two last named. The soil of the region was dry and rather sandy with rough, broken land toward the mountains in the west, yet the Pawnee were essentially an agricultural people, cultivating corn, beans, squash, and pumpkins. Buffalo and other game was abundant in the early days, and the Pawnee were excellent hunters, their hunting expeditions covering a wide area.

The first treaty between the Government of the United States and the Pawnee Indians was made at St. Louis Trading Post in June, 1818.[2]

---

[1] In the classification of the North American races by John W. Powell the Pawnee is classified as one of the five independent groups of the Caddoan stock. Miss Alice C. Fletcher regards the Pawnee as a confederacy, the divisions or bands of the tribe being treated by her as separate tribes in the Handbook of American Indians North of Mexico, Bull. 30, Bur. Amer. Ethn., pt. 2, p 213. Cf. also Linton, Ralph, The Thunder Ceremony of the Pawnee, The Sacrifice to the Morning Star by the Skidi Pawnee, and Annual Ceremony of the Pawnee Medicine Men, compiled chiefly from unpublished notes of Dr. G. A. Dorsey, published as leaflets Nos. 5, 6, and 8, Field Museum of Natural History, Chicago, 1922-23.

[2] Indian Affairs; Laws and Treaties, Charles J. Kappler, ed., vol. II, pp. 156-159, Washington, 1904.

1

At that time a separate treaty was made with each band of Pawnee, designated as Grand, Noisy, Republic, and Marhar, the treaties being respectively on June 18, 19, 20, and 22. Peace was then concluded with all tribes of the region which had been disturbed by the war of 1812. A treaty with the Pawnee Tribe was made at Fort Atkinson, Council Bluffs, September 30, 1825, its purpose being "to remove all future cause of discussion or dissension." [3] By the treaty of October 9, 1833, the Pawnee ceded to the United States "all the land lying south of the Platt River." [4] A reservation in Nebraska was provided for the Pawnee who remained in that State until 1876, the sale of their reservation in Nebraska being approved on June 5 of that year. The setting apart of a reservation in Indian Territory (Oklahoma) was approved April 10, 1876. The Pawnee were removed to that reservation and "each head of a family or single person over 21 years of age residing upon said reserve, who shall so elect," was entitled to receive an allotment of 160 acres of land.[5] In a table compiled by the Office of Indian Affairs in 1908 it is stated that "112,859.84 acres were allotted to 821 [Pawnee] Indians, 840 acres reserved for school, agency, and cemetery purposes, and the residue of 169,320 acres was opened to settlement," the agreement being ratified by act of March 3, 1893.[6]

The number of Pawnee in 1702 was estimated by Iberville at 2,000 families. In 1838 they numbered about 10,000 persons, but the opening of a principal emigrant trail directly through the country in the forties introduced disease and dissipation and left the people less able to defend themselves against their enemies, the Sioux.[7] They decreased in numbers and in 1928 the Pawnee population was 2,766.[8]

The reservation of the Pawnee is beautifully diversified, with many streams and tracts of woods. There are outcroppings of stone in the region south of the town of Pawnee (pl. 3, *a*, *b*) while north of the town are broad, smooth fields. (Pl. 3. *c*.) On a private ranch near Pawnee a picturesque herd of buffalo was seen near a "buffalo wallow." (Pl. 4, *a*, *b*.)

The earth lodge of the Pawnee was about 40 feet in diameter and 15 feet high, and was occupied by several related families, each having its appointed space along the wall. "At the west side of the lodge a space was always reserved, which was considered sacred, and was called *wiharu* (place-for-the-wonderful-things), this being the name which is applied to the garden of the Evening Star, where the corn is always ripening and where are stored many parflêches of buffalo

[3] Ibid., pp. 258–260.
[4] Ibid., pp. 416–418.
[5] Ibid., vol. I, pp. 159–161.
[6] Handbook of American Indians, Bull. 30, Bur. Amer. Ethn., pt. 2, p. 383.
[7] Ibid., p. 216.
[8] Report of the Bureau of Indian Affairs for the year 1928, p. 58.

a, Landscape south of Pawnee, Okla.

b, Landscape south of Pawnee, Okla.

c, Landscape north of Pawnee, Okla.

a, "Buffalo wallow" on private ranch near Pawnee, Okla.

b, Buffalo grazing on private ranch near Pawnee, Okla.

meat. Here rested a buffalo skull, so placed that it faced the entrance of the lodge and, consequently, the rising sun. Above this, and suspended from one of the rafter poles, was the sacred bundle and other religious paraphernalia."[9] This space is designated as the altar, and the sleeping space on either side of it was the most honored, the positions being graduated downward to that of the oldest people, which was next the door. The floor of the lodge was a foot or two below the ground and its framework may briefly be described as a "skeleton stockade" of heavy posts on which poles were laid, extending upward to the posts which supported the smoke-hole and outward to a bank of earth around the outer edge of the lodge. This framework was covered with earth and sod, resting on long willow rods laid transversely on the poles or rafters. The entrance was protected by a covered way built of poles and having an earth-covered roof. This lodge was constructed in a ceremonial manner and when a family returned from an absence the posts of the lodge were ceremonially anointed before they resumed their occupancy. A family usually possessed also a tipi covered with hides and used as a summer abode while on the hunt. Another structure used on the hunt was made by bending willows into a dome-like frame which was covered with boughs or skins.

The tribal organization has been mentioned as consisting of four bands, each living in its own location. Each band had its hereditary chief and its council composed of the chief and leading men. It had also its shrine ("sacred bundle") containing sacred objects, and its priests who had charge of the rituals and ceremonies connected with those objects. Miss Fletcher states that "Through the sacred and symbolic articles of the shrines and their rituals and ceremonies a medium of communication was believed to be opened between the people and the supernatural powers by which food, long life, and prosperity were obtained."[10]

The social organization of the tribe was clearly defined. At the head of this social order stood the chief, whose orders were enforced by four men called Nahikuts. Below these in rank were the Kurahus or priests who performed the ceremonies; next in order were the Kurau, or medicine men, and the warriors, while below these were the members of the tribe who held no office. The tribal council was composed of men who belonged to the council of several bands, and this body transacted all business which affected the welfare of the tribe. Descent was reckoned through the female line, and a man, after his marriage, went to live with his wife's family.

---

[9] Dorsey, George A. Traditions of the Skidi Pawnee. Memoirs Amer. Folk-Lore Society, vol. VIII, p. xv, New York, 1904.

[10] Handbook of American Indians, Bull. 30, Bur. Amer. Ethn., pt. 2, p. 215.

The medicine men claimed to have received their power from supernatural sources and were organized into numerous societies. Linton states that "The function of the medicine men's ceremonies was threefold. By them they renewed their powers, drove disease from the village, and, by means of their sleight-of-hand performances, convinced the people that they really possessed the supernatural powers attributed to them." [a]

According to Miss Fletcher their "religious ceremonies were connected with the cosmic forces and the heavenly bodies. The dominating power was Tirawa, generally spoken of as 'father.' The heavenly bodies, the winds, thunder, lightning, and rain were his messengers. . . . The mythology of the Pawnee is remarkably rich in symbolism and poetic fancy, and their religious system is elaborate and cogent. The secret societies, of which there were several in each tribe, were connected with the belief in supernatural animals. The functions of these societies were to call the game, to heal diseases, and to give occult powers. Their rites were elaborate and their ceremonies dramatic." [11] Next in power to Tirawa was Evening Star, regarded as a woman, and below her was Morning Star, a warrior who drove the other stars before him across the sky. The child of these two deities was the first human being. In the west, Evening Star had a beautiful garden with fields of ripening corn and many buffalo, and from this garden sprang all the streams of life.

Next in rank to Evening Star and Morning Star were the gods of the four world-quarters who supported the heavens and who stood in the northeast, southeast, southwest and northwest, these being the sacred directions of the Pawnee. Dorsey states that "next to these gods in rank are the three gods of the north, supreme among whom is the North-Star, Karariwari (One-who-does-not-move). Associated with him are Hutukawahar (Wind-ready-to-give) and Hikus (Breath). The North-Star is . . . symbolic of the chief . . . while his assistants, equally beneficent, sent the buffalo and the breath of life." [12] Below these in turn were Sun and Moon, from whose union sprang the second human being on the earth. This daughter, marrying the son of Morning Star and Evening Star, produced the human race.

The lesser gods of the heavens included Star of the South and Big-black-meteoric-star, who was the god of the medicine men. There were also earth gods organized into four lodges, each with its leaders and messengers, these gods being the special patrons of warriors and medicine men.

---

[a] Linton, Ralph. Annual ceremony of the Pawnee medicine men, Field Museum of Natural History, Leaflet No. 8, Chicago, 1923, pp. 19, 20.

[11] Handbook of American Indians, Bull. 30, Bur. Amer. Ethn., pt. 2, p. 215.

[12] Dorsey, op. cit., p. XIX.

It was the belief of the Pawnee that all the members of a band were descended from one ancestor, and that the "sacred bundle" belonging to the band (or village community) was given to its ancestor by one of these heavenly beings. In addition to the bundles belonging to the several bands there were two bundles which were the property of the entire tribe. Each of the bundles contained one or two ears of corn, called "Mother Corn," which were the most sacred articles in the group. If two ears of corn were used, one was attached to a stick and symbolized the male element, or Morning Star, while the other symbolized the female element, or Evening Star. These ears of corn were shelled and given to the people as seed corn at the first ceremony in the spring. Next in importance were the tobacco-filled skins of hawks and owls, the hawk skin symbolizing a warrior and the owl skin a chief who must always be awake and watchful. Other articles in every bundle were sweet grass for incense, one or more scalps taken from slain enemies, tobacco, paints, and one or more pipe bowls. Some bundles contained other articles, and the skins of birds other than those mentioned.

The bundle belonging to a band was in charge of an hereditary keeper, and as the bundles were inherited in the female line, the owners were always women. When not in use a bundle was wrapped in buffalo hide, tied with a rope of plaited buffalo hair, and hung on the west wall of the lodge above the buffalo skull which was always placed opposite the entrance of the lodge. (Pl. 5, a.) The Morning Star bundle and its ceremony will be considered in a subsequent paragraph. The beliefs of the Pawnee differed considerably from those of other tribes using sacred bundles and Dr. G. A. Dorsey considers the village bundles of the Pawnee more nearly comparable to the elaborate altars of the Southwest Indians than to the medicine bundles of the northern Plains tribes and central Algonquian.

Elaborate ceremonies were connected with the sacred bundles. The ceremonial year of the Pawnee began with the first thunder in the spring, when the sacred seed corn was given to the people (pl. 7, a),[13] and ended with the harvest ceremony, which was followed by a ceremony known as "Making Mother Corn." At this ceremony the ears of corn in all the sacred bundles were renewed from the freshly gathered harvest. Aside from the seasonal observances there were numerous ceremonies whose time of observance was not fixed. All these were in charge of priests and had the welfare of the people as their object. These ceremonies contained a dramatization of some actions attributed to the gods and in practically all there was

---

[13] The writer acknowledges the courtesy of Dr. J. C. Simms, Director of the Field Meusum of Natural History, in providing this photograph, also those of the sacred bundle and the costumes (pls. 5, a; 8).

some form of offering or sacrifice. In addition to these were the ceremonies of the warrior societies and the medicine men. The number and elaborateness of the ceremonies show the Pawnee to have been, in the old times, a ceremonial people among whom symbolism was highly developed.[14] Only a portion of this rich ceremonialism is considered in the present work.

Peyote is used extensively among the Pawnee at the present time, but the subject was not studied nor its songs recorded. The writer listened to several of the songs, which were simple and appeared to be modern melodies.

---

[14] Cf. Fletcher, Alice C., The Hako, a Pawnee Ceremony. Twenty-second Ann. Rept. Bur. Amer. Ethn., pt. 2, Washington, 1903.

COMPARISON OF PAWNEE SONGS WITH CHIPPEWA, SIOUX, UTE, MANDAN, HIDATSA, AND PAPAGO SONGS

MELODIC ANALYSIS

TABLE 1.—TONALITY

	Chippewa, Sioux, Ute, Mandan, Hidatsa, and Papago	Per cent	Pawnee	Per cent	Total	Per cent
Major tonality_____	520	*53*	33	*38*	553	*51*
Minor tonality_____	424	*42*	39	*46*	463	*43*
Both major and minor_____	5	------	1	*1*	6	------
Third lacking_____	26	*2*	12	*14*	38	*4*
Irregular [1]_____	12	*1*	1	*1*	13	*1*
Total_____	987	------	86	------	1, 073	------

[1] Songs are thus classified if they are "pure melody without tonality," the tones not having an apparent relation to a keynote. In such songs the tones appear to be arranged with reference to intervals rather than with reference to a keynote, many being based on successive intervals of a fourth.

TABLE 2.—FIRST NOTE OF SONG—ITS RELATION TO KEYNOTE

	Chippewa, Sioux, Ute, Mandan, Hidatsa, and Papago	Per cent	Pawnee	Per cent	Total	Per cent
Beginning on the—						
Fourteenth_____	1	------	------	------	1	------
Thirteenth_____	4	------	1	*1*	5	------
Twelfth_____	143	*10*	7	*8*	150	*14*
Eleventh_____	14	*1*	1	*1*	15	*1*
Tenth_____	55	*6*	14	*16*	69	*6*
Ninth_____	28	*3*	4	*5*	32	*3*
Octave_____	199	*20*	17	*20*	216	*20*
Seventh_____	16	*2*	------	------	16	*1*
Sixth_____	34	*3*	1	*1*	35	*3*
Fifth_____	264	*30*	21	*24*	285	*26*
Fourth_____	17	*2*	2	*2*	19	*2*
Third_____	82	*8*	4	*5*	86	*8*
Second_____	22	*2*	2	*2*	24	*2*
Keynote_____	96	*10*	11	*13*	107	*10*
Irregular_____	12	*1*	1	*1*	13	*1*
Total_____	987	------	86	------	1, 073	------

7

TABLE 3.—LAST NOTE OF SONG—ITS RELATION TO KEYNOTE

	Chippewa, Sioux, Ute, Mandan, Hidatsa, and Papago	Per cent	Pawnee	Per cent	Total	Per cent
Ending on the—						
Sixth	1				1	
Fifth	327	33	21	24	348	32
Third	112	10	2	1	114	11
Keynote	535	54	62	72	597	56
Irregular	12	1	1	1	13	1
Total	987		86		1, 073	

TABLE 4.—LAST NOTE OF SONG—ITS RELATION TO COMPASS

	Chippewa, Sioux, Ute, Mandan, Hidatsa, and Papago	Per cent	Pawnee	Per cent	Total	Per cent
Songs in which final note is—						
Lowest in song	733	74	68	78	801	75
Highest in song	1				1	
Immediately preceded by—						
Fifth below	1				1	
Fourth below	23	2	2	2	25	2
Major third below	7				7	
Minor third below	28	3	1	1	29	3
Whole tone below	19	2	2	2	21	2
Semitone below	7		2	2	9	
Immediately preceded by a lower tone and containing tones lower than final tone	168	17	11	10	179	16
Total	987		86		1, 073	

TABLE 5.—NUMBER OF TONES COMPRISED IN COMPASS OF SONG

	Chippewa, Sioux, Ute, Mandan, Hidatsa, and Papago	Per cent	Pawnee	Per cent	Total	Per cent
Seventeen tones	3		4	5	7	
Fifteen tones	1				1	
Fourteen tones	15	2			15	1
Thirteen tones	54	5	4	5	58	6
Twelve tones	171	18	10	11	181	17
Eleven tones	82	8	8	9	90	8
Ten tones	111	10	12	14	123	11
Nine tones	103	10	5	6	108	10
Eight tones	284	30	19	22	303	27
Seven tones	62	6	3	3	65	6
Six tones	56	6	7	8	63	6
Five tones	36	4	12	14	48	5
Four tones	6		1	1	7	
Three tones	3		1	1	4	
Total	987		86		1, 073	

TABLE 6.—TONE MATERIAL

	Chippewa, Sioux, Ute, Mandan, Hidatsa, and Papago	Per cent	Pawnee	Per cent	Total	Per cent
First 5-toned scale [1]	13	1	5	6	18	1
Second 5-toned scale	99	10	7	8	106	10
Fourth 5-toned scale	227	20	8	9	235	22
Fifth 5-toned scale	2				2	
Major triad	13	1	1		14	1
Major triad and one other tone	119	14	4		123	20
Minor triad	4				4	
Minor triad and one other tone	86	9	10	11	96	9
Octave complete	58	6	4	5	62	5
Octave complete except seventh	93	9	8	9	101	9
Octave complete except seventh and one other tone	93	9	14	16	107	10

[1] The 5-toned scales mentioned in this table are the 5 pentatonic scales according to Helmholtz, described by him as follows: "1. The first scale, without third or seventh. . . . To the second scale, without second or sixth, belong most Scotch airs which have a minor character. . . The third scale, without third and sixth . . . To the fourth scale, without fourth or seventh, belong most Scotch airs which have the character of a major mode. The fifth scale, without second and fifth." (Helmholtz, H. L., The Sensations of Tone, London, 1885, pp. 260, 261.)

Table 6.—TONE MATERIAL—Continued

	Chippewa, Sioux, Ute, Mandan, Hidatsa, and Papago	Per cent	Pawnee	Per cent	Total	Per cent
Octave complete except sixth_	38	*4*	2	*2*	40	*3*
Octave complete except sixth and one other tone_____	15	*1*	4	*5*	19	*1*
Octave complete except fifth and one other tone_____	1	------	-------	------	1	------
Octave complete except fourth_____	26	*3*	5	*6*	31	*3*
Octave complete except fourth and one other tone_	10	*1*	-------	------	10	*1*
Octave complete except third_	5	------	-------	------	5	------
Octave complete except second_____	27	*3*	-------	------	27	*2*
Other combinations of tone__	58	*6*	14	*16*	72	*6*
Total_____	987	------	86	------	1,073	------

Table 7.—ACCIDENTALS

	Chippewa, Sioux, Ute, Mandan, Hidatsa, and Papago	Per cent	Pawnee	Per cent	Total	Per cent
Songs containing—						
No accidentals_____	822	*85*	78	*92*	900	*84*
Seventh raised a semitone_____	22	*2*	3	*3*	25	*2*
Sixth raised a semitone__	17	*1*	-------	------	17	*1*
Fourth raised a semitone_	20	*2*	2	*2*	22	*2*
Third raised a semitone_	3	------	-------	------	3	------
Third lowered a semitone_____	2	------	-------	------	2	------
Other combinations of tone_____	89	*9*	2	*2*	91	*9*
Irregular_____	12	*1*	1	*1*	13	*1*
Total_____	987	------	86	------	1,073	------

TABLE 8.—STRUCTURE

	Chippewa, Sioux, Ute, Mandan, Hidatsa, and Papago	Per cent	Pawnee	Per cent	Total	Per cent
Melodic	594	*60*	48	*56*	642	*60*
Melodic with harmonic framework	197	*20*	15	*17*	212	*20*
Harmonic	184	*19*	22	*25*	206	*19*
Irregular	12	*1*	1	*1*	13	*1*
Total	987	------	86	------	1,073	------

TABLE 9.—FIRST PROGRESSION—DOWNWARD AND UPWARD

	Chippewa, Sioux, Ute, Mandan, Hidatsa, and Papago	Per cent	Pawnee	Per cent	Total	Per cent
Downward	608	*61*	62	*71*	670	*62*
Upward	379	*38*	24	*28*	403	*38*
Total	987	------	86	------	1,073	------

TABLE 10.—TOTAL NUMBER OF PROGRESSIONS—DOWNWARD AND UPWARD

	Chippewa, Sioux, Ute, Mandan, Hidatsa, and Papago	Per cent	Pawnee	Per cent	Total	Per cent
Downward	16,848	*63*	1,393	*64*	18,241	*63*
Upward	9,929	*37*	786	*36*	10,715	*37*
Total	26,777	------	2,179	------	28,956	------

TABLE 11.—INTERVALS IN DOWNWARD PROGRESSION

	Chippewa, Sioux, Ute, Mandan, Hidatsa, and Papago	Per cent	Pawnee	Per cent	Total	Per cent
Interval of a—						
Twelfth	1	------	------	------	1	------
Ninth	1	------	------	------	1	------
Octave	2	------	2	------	4	------
Seventh	2	------	4	------	6	------
Major sixth	13	------	4	------	17	------
Minor sixth	20	------	10	*1*	30	------
Fifth	138	------	12	*1*	150	------

TABLE 11.—INTERVALS IN DOWNWARD PROGRESSION—Continued

	Chippewa, Sioux, Ute, Mandan, Hidatsa, and Papago	Per cent	Pawnee	Per cent	Total	Per cent
Interval of a—Continued.						
Fourth	1, 761	10	158	11	1, 919	11
Major third	1, 651	10	139	10	1, 790	10
Minor third	5, 099	30	322	24	5, 421	30
Augmented second	8				8	
Major second	7, 553	46	635	45	8, 188	45
Minor second	599	3	107	1	706	3
Total	16, 848		1, 393		18, 241	

TABLE 12.—INTERVALS IN UPWARD PROGRESSION

	Chippewa, Sioux, Ute, Mandan, Hidatsa, and Papago	Per cent	Pawnee	Per cent	Total	Per cent
Interval of a—						
Fourteenth	1				1	
Twelfth	17				17	
Eleventh	4		1		5	
Tenth	14		2		16	
Ninth	15		2		17	
Octave	136	1	19	2	155	1
Seventh	40		2		42	
Major sixth	122	1	16	2	138	1
Minor sixth	82	1	20	2	102	1
Fifth	645	6	65	8	710	7
Fourth	1, 686	17	112	14	1, 798	17
Major third	1, 068	10	74	9	1, 142	10
Minor third	2, 489	25	119	14	2, 608	24
Major second	3, 267	33	286	37	3, 553	33
Minor second	343	3	68	9	411	4
Total	9, 929		786		10, 715	

TABLE 13—AVERAGE NUMBER OF SEMITONES IN AN INTERVAL

	Chippewa, Sioux, Ute, Mandan, Hidatsa, and Papago	Per cent	Pawnee	Per cent	Total	Per cent
Number of songs	987		86		1, 073	
Number of intervals	26, 777		2, 179		28, 956	
Number of semitones	82, 664		6, 856		89, 520	
Average number of semitones in an interval	3. 08		3. 18		3. 26	

RHYTHMIC ANALYSIS

TABLE 14.—PART OF MEASURE ON WHICH SONG BEGINS

	Chippewa, Sioux, Ute, Mandan, Hidatsa, and Papago	Per cent	Pawnee	Per cent	Total	Per cent
Beginning on unaccented part of measure	354	36	42	50	396	37
Beginning on accented part of measure	591	60	44	50	635	58
Transcribed in outline	42	4			42	4
Total	987		86		1,073	

TABLE 15.—RHYTHM (METER) OF FIRST MEASURE

	Chippewa, Sioux, Ute, Mandan, Hidatsa, and Papago	Per cent	Pawnee	Per cent	Total	Per cent
First measure in—						
2–4 time	539	54	54	62	593	55
3–4 time	356	36	28		384	37
4–4 time	9	1			9	1
5–4 time	13	1	2		15	1
6–4 time	1				1	
7–4 time	2				2	
3–8 time	7				7	
4–8 time	6				6	
5–8 time	8		1		9	
6–8 time	1				1	
7–8 time	1				1	
2–2 time	2		1		3	
Transcribed in outline	42	4			42	4
Total	987		86		1,073	

TABLE 16.—CHANGE OF TIME (MEASURE LENGTHS)

	Chippewa, Sioux, Ute, Mandan, Hidatsa, and Papago	Per cent	Pawnee	Per cent	Total	Per cent
Songs containing no change of time	134	10	22	26	156	14
Songs containing a change of time	811	84	64	74	875	81
Transcribed in outline	42	4			42	4
Total	987		86		1,073	

TABLE 17.—RHYTHMIC UNIT

	Chippewa, Sioux, Ute, Mandan, Hidatsa, and Papago	Per cent	Pawnee	Per cent	Total	Per cent
Songs containing—						
No rhythmic unit_____	305	*30*	13	*15*	318	*30*
One rhythmic unit_____	524	*53*	40	*46*	564	*52*
Two rhythmic units_____	96	*10*	26	*30*	122	*11*
Three rhythmic units____	13	*1*	7	*8*	20	*2*
Four rhythmic units_____	5	_____	_____	_____	5	_____
Five rhythmic units_____	2	_____	_____	_____	2	_____
Transcribed in outline_____	42	*4*	_____	_____	42	*4*
Total_____	987	_____	86	_____	1, 073	_____

DESCRIPTIVE ANALYSIS

TABLE 1.—The distinctive structure of Pawnee songs is shown in this table. The percentage of songs with minor tonality is 46. This is higher than in any tribe under anaylsis except the Sioux, which has 60 per cent of its songs in minor tonality. The percentage of songs lacking the third above the keynote is 14, contrasted with 10 per cent in the Papago and 1 in the other tribes. One song is classified as irregular, and one as both major and minor in tonality.

TABLE 2.—The highest percentages of initial tones are on the tenth, octave, fifth, and keynote, showing that the fundamental and its simplest overtones are used for the framework of a majority of the melodies. The percentage of songs beginning on the tenth is 16, while the highest in any other tribe (the Sioux) is 10 per cent. In the songs beginning on the octave this tribe shows the same percentage as the total of 987 songs previously analyzed, while in those beginning on the fifth the percentage is considerably below that tabulation. Only 5 per cent of the songs begin on the third, while the total number shows 8 per cent beginning on that tone, but the percentage beginning on the keynote is 13, contrasted with 10 in the other tribes. Pawnee songs therefore differ from tribes previously analyzed in having a much higher percentage beginning on the tenth and the keynote, and a lower percentage beginning on the fifth and third, while having the same percentage beginning on the octave.

TABLE 3.—A preference for the keynote is shown in this, as in the preceding table, the percentage ending on the keynote being 72 while in the tribes previously analyzed it is only 54. Similarly, an avoidance of the third is shown in the ending of 1 per cent of the songs on that tone while the total of songs from other tribes shows 10 per cent ending on that tone.

TABLE 4.—The difference between the songs in various tribes is clearly shown in this table. In the Pawnee songs 78 per cent end on the lowest tone of the compass, while in the Papago group 90 per cent contain tones lower than the final tone. The Papago resemble the Chippewa and Sioux, which have respectively 90 and 88 per cent ending on the lowest tone of the compass.

TABLE 5.—In the compass of the songs we again see a feeling for the overtones of a fundamental, the highest percentage being those having a compass of 12, 10, 8, and 5 tones. The percentage having a range of an octave is smaller than in any tribe except the Chippewa, while the percentage with a compass of 5 tones is 14, the largest in any tribe under present consideration. This is approached only by the Mandan and Hidatsa, with 8 per cent.

TABLE 6.—The major and minor 5-toned scales are not favored by the Pawnee, only 23 per cent of their songs being based on these scales, while in the 987 songs previously analyzed 31 per cent are based on these scales. Five of these songs are on the first 5-toned scale which omits the third and seventh tones of the diatonic octave. The Pawnee avoid the use of the complete octave, showing only 5 per cent of such songs, while the entire number of other songs show 6 per cent. It is, however, interesting to note that 38 per cent of the Pawnee songs contain the octave lacking one or two tones, while the combined songs of other tribes show only 30 per cent of such melodies. Thus it is shown that the Pawnee have a smaller percentage of songs on the 5-toned scales and the complete octave, and a much larger percentage containing six or seven tones. This suggests a less primitive form of music than that based on 5-toned scales.

TABLE 7.—The percentage of songs without accidentals is larger than in any other tribe under analysis except the Ute, which contains 96 per cent of such melodies. The most frequent accidental is the seventh raised a semitone, this occurring in three songs which are minor in tonality.

TALBE 8.—In structure we find the harmonic songs higher in percentage than in any tribe except the Mandan and Hidatsa, which comprise 30 per cent of such songs. The Pawnee comprise 25 per cent. This shows a less primitive structure in Pawnee than in the other songs under analysis, a majority of which are melodic in structure.

TABLE 9.—The percentage of songs beginning with a downward progression is considerably higher than in any other tribe under analysis. The percentage in Pawnee is 71, while in the Papago songs it is only 37, and in the Mandan and Hidatsa songs it is 51 per cent.

TABLE 10.—The percentage of descending and ascending intervals is almost the same in the Pawnee as in the combined Chippewa, Sioux, Ute, Mandan, Hidatsa, and Papago songs, the percentage in the combined tribes being 63 in descending and 37 in ascending intervals, while the Pawnee contain 64 per cent descending and 36 per cent ascending intervals. This, like the preceding table, shows the descending trend of Pawnee songs. A different trend is shown in the Papago songs, which contain 59 per cent descending and 41 per cent ascending intervals.

TABLES 11 AND 12.—A peculiarity of Pawnee songs is shown in the relatively small percentage of minor thirds, these being 24 per cent in descending and 14 per cent in ascending progression, contrasted with 30 and 25 per cent in the combined songs of other tribes. The Pawnee, more than other tribes, use the interval of a fifth which constitutes 1 per cent of the descending and 8 per cent of the ascending intervals but which, in the combined other tribes, constitutes less than 1 per cent of the descending and 6 per cent of the ascending intervals. The fourth occurs with about the same frequency in Pawnee as in the other tribes but the percentage of whole tones is 45 in descending and 37 in ascending order, contrasted with 46 per cent in descending and only 33 per cent in ascending order. The percentage of semitones (both ascending and descending) is 10 in the Pawnee and only 6 in the other tribes under analysis.

TABLE 13.—The average number of semitones in an interval is slightly larger than in the Ute, which was 3.14 semitones, and considerably larger than in the combined songs under analysis, which is 3.08 semitones. The average interval is still approximately a minor third, and contains 3.18 semitones.

TABLE 14.—In all the tribes previously studied a majority of the songs have begun on the accented part of the measure. The Pawnee songs are evenly divided in this respect, half beginning on the accented and half on the unaccented part of the measure.

TABLE 15.—The Pawnee resemble the other tribes under observation in preferring to begin their songs in 2–4 time rather than in triple or other meter. The Papago songs show 66 per cent and the Ute and Pawnee each 62 per cent beginning in double time. In other tribes the percentage of songs beginning in 2–4 time is smaller.

TABLE 16.—In the percentage of songs containing no change of time the Pawnee is higher than any other tribe under analysis, showing 26 per cent. The nearest approach to this is the Chippewa with 23 per cent and the lowest is the Papago with only 9 per cent. The Chippewa Tribe has probably been in contact with the music of the white race more than any other analyzed tribe except the Pawnee, and a modification is clearly shown in the retaining of one measure-length throughout so large a proportion of the songs.

TABLE 17.—A developed rhythmic structure is shown in the high percentage of songs containing two rhythmic units, this being 30 per cent in the Pawnee and only 10 per cent in the combined songs of other tribes. The songs with three rhythmic units constitute 8 per cent in the Pawnee and 1 per cent in the songs of other tribes. The percentage of Pawnee songs with one rhythmic unit is considerably lower than in the combined tribes and that of the songs with no rhythmic unit is only half the percentage in the larger group.

The comparative table showing the rhythm of the drum has been discontinued, as the purpose of this analysis seems to have been accomplished. The analysis of Pawnee songs according to this basis is shown on page 125. This data and the comparative table of drum rhythms in Bulletin 80, pages 25–26, show that the Indians under observation prefer an even drumbeat, each stroke uniform in stress and corresponding to sixteenth, eighth, quarter, or half notes of the song. In some tribes there have been instances of elaborate drumbeats, but no trace of this was found among the Pawnee, either in recorded songs or in the performances heard at gatherings. This is in accordance with other evidence that the music of the Pawnee has been modified by the establishing of a more settled mode of life or, perhaps, by hearing the music of the white race. The Yuma and Cocopa, in contrast to these tribes, use elaborate rhythms of drum and rattle.

Other tables which have been discontinued are those showing the keynote of the song and the metronome tempo of voice and drum. These were last used in the analysis of 710 songs in Northern Ute Music, Bulletin 75, pages 42 and 48–51. The result of the analysis was summarized in Mandan and Hidatsa Music, Bulletin 80, page 15.

SUMMARY

From the foregoing it appears that Pawnee songs resemble those of the Ute more closely than those of other tribes. Occasional resemblances are noted between the Pawnee and Chippewa, as well as between the Pawnee and Sioux, Mandan, and Hidatsa, but the Pawnee songs differ widely from those of the Papago who live on the Mexican border, a portion of the tribe still residing in Mexico.

The statement has been made in a previous paragraph that certain results of the Pawnee analyses suggest the influence of a settled mode of life or a contact with the music of civilization. This should not be understood to mean that the form of all the songs has been changed. This work contains many songs that undoubtedly have come down for many generations and there is no reason to think they were not sung correctly, but there are also songs of more recent origin, recorded in order that the music of the entire tribe may be represented. All these songs are combined in the analyses and the latter class, to some extent, affects the total numbers.

An important point, made evident in this comparative analysis, is the individuality of Pawnee music. It is distinct, in its entirety, from the songs of other tribes, though bearing a resemblance to one tribe or another in separate characteristics. The study of Indian music by an established system of analysis shows there are characteristics that are common to Indian songs of various tribes and different from the music of the white race, and also characteristics which distinguish the songs of one tribe from those of another. Among the former is the change of measure-lengths found in many Indian songs and the downward trend of the melody. The latter are indicated in the foregoing paragraphs. A characteristic of Pawnee music that evades, to some extent, the tabulated analysis, is its simplicity of both melody and rhythm. This can only be appreciated by a study of the melodies themselves. Pawnee music is the plainest of any thus far recorded in its rhythmic divisions and general content. This characteristic of the group may, however, be due to the absence of songs used in treating the sick, which are usually songs of complicated rhythms.

MORNING STAR CEREMONY

A sacred bundle of the Skidi Pawnee was associated with Morning Star and its ceremony was held in the early spring, having for its object the securing of good crops in the coming season. It was the writer's privilege to see the Morning Star bundle in the house of the woman who was its keeper, and also to see its contents exposed in the ceremony. The bundle, in accordance with custom, was hung on the west wall of its owner's house, and with it were hung four large gourds, symbolizing the four deities who were the special guardians of Evening Star and also representing the breasts of the two women in the west, Evening Star and Moon.[15]

The legend from which the Morning Star ceremony arose was related by Coming Sun, whose grandfather was a high priest in the Morning Star village and who received his name by inheritance from this ancestor. With Coming Sun's narrative is combined a limited number of details mentioned by Linton in "Sacrifice to the Morning Star by the Skidi Pawnee."

As already stated, Morning Star ruled in the east and Evening Star in the west. All the stars west of the Milky Way were feminine and those to the east were masculine, but the most powerful were Morning Star and Evening Star. Sun was with the former and Moon was a companion of the latter. One after another the eastern

---

[15] Cf. Dorsey, Traditions of the Skidi Pawnee, pp. 52–55.

stars came to court the stars in the west, in order that man might be placed on the earth. Moon welcomed them and walked with them toward the west, but as soon as they came in sight of the village she caused the ground to open so the man fell through and was killed. At last Morning Star resolved to go and woo the great Evening Star, taking his little brother along to carry his pack. Thus, according to Coming Sun, a small star always appears near and slightly below the morning star in the spring, representing the little brother. Linton, however, states that Morning Star was accompanied by Sun, who carried a sacred bundle with a war club.

Ten obstacles were encountered by Morning Star and his companion, the first five being difficulties of travel, such as sharp flints and sword grass beneath their feet, and the last five being animals which attacked them, including the mountain lion, wildcat, buffalo, and bear. All these were placed in their way by Moon, who thought she could conquer them as she had conquered the others. But Morning Star carried a ball encased in such a manner that when he threw it the casing broke and it became a ball of fire. When throwing the ball he sang the following song, which was said to be one of the principal songs in the ceremony. Linton states that Morning Star struck the ground with his war club, closing the cracks made by Moon for his destruction, and that he sang a song with substantially the same words recorded by Coming Sun.

No. 1. Song of Morning Star   (Catalogue No. 1162)

Sung by COMING SUN

Manner of rendition

FREE TRANSLATION

"This I did when I became angry, in order that in the future the earth might be formed." In later use the words "And I imitate this power" were added, referring to the persons using the song.

Analysis.—This song was considered too sacred for phonographic recording and was orally taught to the writer by Coming Sun. For this reason the metronome time is not indicated. The manner of singing this and other ceremonial songs is indicated in the transcription, one voice singing the opening phrase, and holding a low tone while two or three voices repeat the opening phrase, after which all the voices proceed in unison. This melody is an example of interval formation. The only tones are F, G, B flat, and C, and the principal progressions are whole tones between B flat and C, and between F and G. A similar melodic form occurs in Nos. 5 and 53. This song is transcribed with the signature of the key of F and classified with songs lacking the third above the keynote. The repetitions of the rhythmic unit are six in number and comprise the entire melody. Slight differences in the note values of the rhythmic unit occur in the latter part of the song.

The tenth obstacle was not encountered by Morning Star until after he entered the lodge of Evening Star. The obstacle was a snake, but he overcame it, as he had overcome the others, by means of the ball of fire and the song.

Evening Star saw that his power was greater than hers, but she determined to hold him aloof as long as possible. Finally she insisted that he make provision for the child that should be born; she even required him to provide perfumed water for bathing the child and a cradle board in which it should be placed. On the hoop, or arch, of this cradle board was painted a morning star and the lightnings, this custom being followed by the Pawnee at the present time. Evening Star also required him to plant a tree in front of the lodge so that the mocking birds might nest there and sing to the child. From this union a daughter was born. She came down to earth and wandered about in fear. As she was running hither and thither she met a boy, the child of Sun and Moon, and these two became the ancestors of the human race.

Morning Star made a bundle and placed in it various articles connected with the obstacles he had overcome on his westward journey. He left this bundle with Evening Star and for that reason a woman has always been the keeper of the sacred bundle. Other articles have been added from time to time and will be noted in this paper.

It is said that Evening Star required a human sacrifice as her reward. This sacrifice must be a pure and beautiful maiden and she demanded that the sacrifice be repeated annually. Long ago, Morning Star sometimes appeared to a man in a dream and told him to secure a maiden for this sacrifice. According to Linton, a man who had this vision went to the keeper of the Morning Star bundle and received the warrior's costume and the sacred objects kept for such an expedition. Other warriors joined him and, preliminary to the expedition, they enacted the journey of the Morning Star, and sang the song with which he overcame the obstacles placed in his way. (Cf. Song No. 1.) When the ceremony ended it was almost time for the Morning Star to rise and the leader went outside the lodge and addressed an invocation to him. After dancing furiously around their fire and offering a last prayer to Morning Star the warriors started forth and captured a maiden from the enemy. Returning, they gave her into the care of the chief of the Morning Star village until the time for her sacrifice. She was treated in a ceremonial manner but kept in ignorance of her fate. At the appointed time her body was painted, half red and half black, and she was tied to a scaffold and shot through the heart with an arrow. It was said that the braided thong used to bind the girl to the scaffold is now in the Morning Star bundle.

Tradition states that on one occasion the intended victim was rescued. On the night preceding her execution she was seated beside some tall sunflowers. A young chief came through the tall weeds and stole her away, putting her on his horse and taking her to Fort Leavenworth, whence she was returned to her own people. She died within three months, having been anointed for death with the sacred ointment of red paint powder and buffalo fat. This occurred about the year 1818. The man who rescued the intended victim was a warrior of distinction and through his influence the custom was discontinued. The ritual of the sacrifice is still rendered but no actual sacrifice has taken place since that date.

Coming Sun, who sings the ceremonial songs, said that sometimes, during the Morning Star ceremony he stops and says "Listen," and the people hear a woman's voice singing the songs above his head.

The Morning Star ceremony was held by the Skidi Band near Pawnee, Okla., on April 17, 1920. This ceremony formerly lasted four days and nights, ending when the morning star appeared in the east, but at the present time it is concluded in one day. On this occasion the writer had the honor of entering the lodge, through the courtesy of Coming Sun. It is said that only one other white person, Dr. G. A. Dorsey, has entered the lodge during the ceremony and seen the contents of the sacred bundle.

The ceremony was held in a tipi erected for the occasion in a quiet spot near the house of the keeper of the bundle, north of Pawnee. This tipi had been used in the Ghost dance and was decorated with Ghost dance symbols. (Pl. 5, b.) The adjacent landscape is shown in Plate 3, c. The ceremony began at about 9 a. m. and continued until 4 p. m., the writer sitting outside the tipi except for the brief time she was permitted to enter. Thus the entire songs of the ceremony were heard, as well as the prayers and rituals, though only the principal song was obtained. At the proper time Coming Sun, who was in charge of the ceremony, sent a messenger to summon the writer and she entered the lodge, passing to the right and standing near the bundle, before which she laid gifts of calico, tobacco, and money. Coming Sun was seated back of the bundle, directly opposite the entrance, and held one of the sacred gourd rattles. Two men at either side of him held similar rattles. In front of the men at Coming Sun's left and next the sacred bundle was a belt decorated with human scalps, a coiled thong of braided hide and a bundle of "song-sticks." At the right of the bundle were four owls. The outer wrapping of the bundle is of buffalo hide and this was spread on the ground. On this was a wolf hide, and on the wolf hide lay a pipe, the "Cheyenne arrow," and wildcat paws filled with native tobacco. Between the wolf skin and the fire was a decorated ear of corn fastened to a stick which was stuck in the ground, the tip inclined toward the sacred bundle. This was "Mother Corn" and the decoration consisted of dark lines partly down its length and a white feather and dark streamer at its tip. It is said that the paws of the wildcat are selected to hold the tobacco because the animal is spotted like the star-strewn heavens, and that for the same reason the skin of the wildcat is often used as a wrapping for infants. In accepting the gifts offered by the writer, Coming Sun stroked her arm, accepting them in the prescribed ceremonial manner. She then left the lodge as she had entered, avoiding the space between the bundle and the fire. About 20 men were in the ceremonial lodge. They wore no clothing above the waist and their bodies were smeared with the "sacred paint" made of red paint powder mixed with buffalo fat and kept in the sacred bundle. A large fire was kept burning in the middle of the lodge, although the day was intensely hot.

The woman who kept the bundle prepared the feast that was served early in the afternoon, bringing for the purpose an armful of wooden bowls and a quantity of horn spoons of various sizes strung on a hide thong. The feast consisted chiefly of dried meat, boiled in the usual manner.

The tradition concerning the "Cheyenne arrow" in the Morning Star bundle is as follows: The Skidi were once on a buffalo hunt and were camped in the usual order, the tipis containing the Evening Star bundle and the Skull bundle being on the west side of the circle and that containing the Morning Star bundle being on the east side. The Cheyenne attacked the camp and Big Eagle, who was in charge of the Morning Star bundle, went out to fight. He did not, however, forget his duties, and before going to fight he told the people to close the tipi in which the bundle was kept. He fought well and captured four Cheyenne arrows, one white, one red, one yellow, and one black. The people believed he did this by the power of the Morning Star and the arrows were accordingly placed in the bundle. Afterwards the Cheyenne recovered two arrows by treachery, and another tribe secured one arrow, but the principal arrow is still in the bundle. It is black and has a flint tip. The shaft is of heavy wood, said to have been obtained in Arizona. It is said that the longer the arrow is kept the straighter and heavier it becomes.[16]

---

[16] Cf. Dorsey, George A., "How the Pawnee captured the Cheyenne medicine arrows," Amer. Anthrop., n. s. vol. v, pp. 644–658, Lancaster, 1903.

BUFFALO DANCE

The ceremony of Painting the Buffalo Skull is held every spring by' the Chaui Band of Pawnee and is in charge of Mr. Stacy Matlock, a prominent member of that band. The closing events of the ceremony are the Buffalo and Lance dances, which were witnessed by the writer through the courtesy of Mr. Matlock, no other white person being present. The ceremony and dances were held in a large earth lodge, several miles south of the town of Pawnee. (Pl. 6, *a*, *b*, *c*.) The opening of the lodge was toward the east. At some distance was a framework, probably that of a sweat lodge. (Pl. 7, *b*.) Only members of the Buffalo Society were admitted to the painting of the skull, but during the Buffalo dance the skull, painted a few days previously, lay on a folded blanket in front of the "altar" which was opposite the entrance. This occasion and the Lance dance held a few days later afforded exceptional opportunities to listen to Pawnee songs, but the semidarkness of the lodge and the solemnity of the occasion precluded the taking of notes upon either the music or the details of the ceremonial dances.

The chief singer at both of these dances was Wicita Blain, a blind man who received the songs by inheritance. He led the songs which were sung at a certain position back of the altar. At a later time he recorded the ceremonial songs here presented, also certain songs of the Bear dance, which is held in equally high esteem by the Pawnee. John Luwak, chief of the Chaui Band, was prominent at the Lance dance and later recorded numerous songs, including those of the Crow Lance Society. (Pl. 2, *a*.)

The following song was led by Mr. Blain at the Buffalo dance attended by the writer and is a very old song concerning Mrs. Blain's uncle, whose name was Naru'dapadi. A great herd of buffalo came to the place where the Indians were encamped and threatened the destruction of the village. Her uncle rode toward them, shouting and firing his gun in an attempt to divert them from their course, but he was caught in the herd. There were buffalo on all sides of him as the herd swept through the camp and across a stream, carrying him with them.

Analysis.—This song is minor in tonality and contains all the tones of the octave except the fourth and sixth. These are the tones omitted in the fourth 5-toned scale which is major while the present song is minor in tonality. It is interesting to note that 25 per cent of the intervals are fourths. This interval, in songs of other tribes, has been found to characterize songs associated with motion or connected with animals. The most frequent interval is the whole tone. This song has a compass of 11 tones and contains the fourth below the final tone. Table 4 shows that the final tone is the lowest tone in a majority of the Indian songs under analysis.

a, Sacred bundle

b, Tipi in which Morning Star ceremony was held

a, Exterior of earth lodge in which Buffalo and Lance dances were held

b, Entrance to earth lodge in which Buffalo and Lance dances were held

c, Interior of ceremonial earth lodge, showing "altar"

No. 2. "The Herd Passes Through the Village"

(Catalogue No. 1114)

Recorded by WICITA BLAIN

Voice ♩ ＝ 88
Drum ♩ ＝ 120
See drum-rhythm below

Ti wa-ka ọ we re ru tī ka-ku 'sa— kū-ra ra wa-

kū-ru sa— we re ru tī ka-ku sa ạ ạ—

we ra rī tu-ru kàt-kạ ạ ạ— we re rā hu ka-tā-ta

ru te wī kaks ā-wa-hu ŋ— we re ru tī ka-ku sa a ạ—

we ra rī tu-ru kàt-ka ạ ạ— we re rā hu ka-tā-ta

Drum-rhythm

♪ ♪ ♪ ♪ ♪ ♪

Tī	waka	we	re	ru	tī	kaku	sa
He	said	now	it	do	it	sit among	come
kūra	ra	wakūru					
his	have	sayings					
we	ra	rī	turu	kàtka			
now	have	it	village	cut across			
we	re	rā	hu	katāta	ru	te	
now	they	have	stream	crossed	do	it	
wī	kaks	āwahu					
fly	shout	here and there					

FREE TRANSLATION

Listen, he said,
Now it (the man) sits among them (the buffalo),
These are his sayings,
Now it sits among them as they come,
Now they have passed through the village,
Now they have crossed the stream,
It flies above them here and there, shouting and calling.

The next is considered one of the most valuable of the Buffalo dance songs. It was said to be concerning a buffalo and a crow. The buffalo heard the call of the crow and looked around thinking it might be an enemy, but he was not afraid of the crow.

Analysis.—The change of metric unit from a quarter to an eighth note is clear in all renditions of this song, the time being maintained with special regularity in the 5–8 and 7–8 measures. The first phase is introductory in character, and the dotted eighth notes at the beginning of the third and fourth measures give an effect of vigor to the opening of the song. No rhythmic unit occurs, the changes in measure-lengths giving variety to the rhythm. There is a wide variety of intervals, including a major sixth and a fifth as well as fourths, major and minor thirds and major seconds. The song contains the tones of the fourth 5-toned scale.

No. 3. "The Buffalo and the Crow"

(Catalogue No. 1116)

Recorded by WICITA BLAIN

Voice ♩ = 84 ♪= 168)
Drum ♩ = 84
Drum- rhythm similar to No. 3

Ti wa-ka ra ra ri ke   e   e ku-ra ra ta

wa - kū-ru - ra ___ ri ke a a ti - åts tu ri

rū a a ra_   kā-a-ka_   ra wi kāk-sa   råt-

ku a tu ri   rū a ra a _   ra ___ ri ke a a ti-

åts tu ri   rū a a ra_   kā-a-ka_   rawi kåksa

Tï	waka	ra	rī	ke	kūra	ra	wakūra
He	said	yonder	it	stands	his	have	sayings

tiåts [17]	tu	rī	rū	a	ra	kāka	ra
father	did	it	afraid			crow	did

wī	kāksa	råtku	tu	rī	rū	a	ra
flying	shouting	not real	did	it	afraid		

FREE TRANSLATION

Listen, he said, yonder it stands,
These are his sayings, yonder it stands,
Father (buffalo) was startled,
The crow was flying and shouting but he was not frightened,
He was standing,
Father was startled but not frightened.

---

[17] Tiåts is similar to atïås and åtsi, occurring in other songs.

In the herd was a very old buffalo. He had been lying down and when he tried to rise he fell down again. He was too old and heavy to get up. The next song is concerning this buffalo.

No. 4. "My Dear Father the Buffalo"

(Catalogue No. 1112)

Recorded by WICITA BLAIN

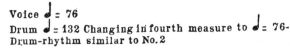

Ha	tī	waka	ēru	tī	átsi [18]	ra	i
Listen	it	said	dear	my	father	have	him
ta	wia		ēru	tī	átsi		witi
do	tell about		dear	my	father		is
ru	ri		wīhaku	sāta	tī		átsi
doing			heavy	going on	my		father

FREE TRANSLATION

Listen, he said,
My dear father (the buffalo),
This is what I was told about it,
He is heavy, he goes on (if he falls he can not rise),
My father (the buffalo).

---

[18] Similar to atiás and tiáts, occurring in other songs.

Analysis.—This song was recorded on two phonographic cylinders, the only difference in the renditions being in the opening phrase. The second renditions were the clearer and the transcription is from that group. The song opens with a three-measure phrase which is designated as a rhythmic unit. This is repeated, and is followed by two phrases in a different rhythm which bring the song to a satisfactory close. Although the song has a compass of 10 tones the largest interval is a fourth. About two-thirds of the progressions are whole tones. The melody contains all the tones of the octave.

An abrupt change in the tempo of the drumbeat occurs in the fourth measure. Other Buffalo and Bear dance songs containing a similar change are Nos. 5, 6, 7, 9, 11, 12, 13, 14, and 15. After this change the drum and voice apparently have the same metric unit but do not always coincide. The metric unit of an Indian's musical performance often contains variations too small to be indicated. Thus in the present instance it can not be said that the drum consistently follows or precedes the voice. The general tempo of each is measured by the metronome and it can only be stated that they do not exactly coincide throughout the renditions of the song.

This and the three songs next following were inherited by the singer from his grandfather and his father. The name of the former was Tida'kawidik (House-full-of-people) and the name of the latter was Kiwi'kude' epaku (Buffalo-fighting). In this song the singer's grandfather is represented as driving the buffalo in the hunt. It was said that he "rode a white horse and frightened the buffalo for other men to shoot."

Analysis.—The change of tempo in the drum is similar to that described with the song next preceding. The drum and voice rarely coincide except on the word *wia*, wherever it occurs. The drumbeat at the close of the song is as follows: The drum ceases after the first stroke on the final syllable of *wia* and begins rapidly at the close of the last measure, continuing in that tempo until the voice begins the repetition of the song. There is no uniformity in the space of time between the renditions of the song. The only tones occurring in this song are D, E, G, and A, and its melodic form resembles that of No. 1. Except for an ascending ninth the only intervals are fourths and whole tones, the latter comprising more than three-fourths of the progressions. The rhythmic unit is long and occupies only a portion of the song.

No. 5. "Yonder the Smoke Was Standing"

(Catalogue No. 1109)

Recorded by WICITA BLAIN

Voice ♩ = 116
Drum ♩ = 132 Changing to ♩ = 116
Drum - rhythm similar to No. 2

| Tĭ | waka | rex | rū | kata | wia | ra | i |
| He | said | him | did | line | coming | have | him |

| tawi | rex | | rū | kata | wia | ra | hū |
| tell about | him | | did | line | coming | have | do |

| kata | wia | rāta | ra | | wis | āriki |
| line | coming | yonder | have | | smoke | standing |

| rex | rū | kata | wia | ra | hū | kata | wia |
| him | did | line | coming | have | do | line | coming |

FREE TRANSLATION

He said, the man was coming along the line,
This is what I was told about it,
He was coming along the line,
Yonder the smoke was standing here and there,
He was coming along the line.

The information concerning the next song is incomplete. It was said the woman who imitated the buffalo was shot through the back but not killed; that she lived a long time afterwards, left Nebraska with the Pawnee Tribe and died in Oklahoma; but the reason for her action is not indicated.

No. 6. "The Woman Imitates the Buffalo"

(Catalogue No. 1110)

Recorded by WICITA BLAIN

Voice ♩ = 80
Drum ♩ = 144 Changing to ♩ = 80
Drum-rhythm similar to No. 2

Ha ti wa-ka ų ē rú rē - a a̲ — ra i ta-we-

a a̲ ų ē̲ ru rē - e - a — tṡa-pȧt tā-ra-ha

tu ra rū - ku e ē ru rē - e - a

e̲ ē ru rē - a ra ū - ra wē ri-ku sa a

Ha	tī	waka	ē	ru	rēa	ra	i
Listen	he	said	yonder	there	her coming	do have	him

tawea	ē	ru	rēa	tsapȧt	tārha
tell about it	yonder	there	her coming	woman	buffalo

tu	ra	rūku	ē	ru	rēa
his	have	imitate	yonder	there	her coming

ra	ūra	wē	riku	sa
have	walk	stopping		coming

FREE TRANSLATION

Listen, he said, yonder she is coming,
This is what I was told about it, yonder she is coming,
The woman imitates the buffalo, yonder she is coming,
She walks, then stops and walks again,
Yonder she is coming.

Analysis.—This melody contains all the tones of the octave except the fourth. It progresses by an unusual variety of intervals, including minor sixths, fourths, major and minor thirds, and major and minor seconds. In structure it is harmonic. It is interesting to note the manner in which the rhythmic unit influences the rhythm of the entire song, although it occurs only three times. There is no change of measure length until near the close of the song, when a triple measure is introduced in a particularly effective manner. The tempo of the drum changes in the fourth measure, as described in No. 4. The four renditions of this song are uniform in every respect.

The next song is concerning a dream of buffalo by the singer's grandfather. He was in his lodge when he saw an animal approaching. In the distance he thought it was a horse, but when it came nearer he saw that it was a buffalo. That night he dreamed of a horse that turned into a buffalo and told him of many good things that would happen to him.

No. 7. "The Buffalo Are Coming"

(Catalogue No. 1115)

Recorded by WICITA BLAIN

Voice ♩ = 96
Drum ♩ = 138 Changing to ♩ = 96
Drum-rhythm similar to No. 2

Ha ti wa-ka i tā-ra-ha ha — rē ra

kū - ra ra wa-kū-e-ru tā - ra-ha— rē ra tā-

ra - ha— rē ra tā-ra - ha— rē ra tā-ra-ha a rē ra

ra ū - ra wē ri-ku sa tā-ra' - ha ha— rē ra tā-

ra - ha— rē ra tā-ra-ha— rē ra tā-ra-ha a rē ra

Ha	tī	waka	tāraha	rē	ra	kūra
Listen	he	said	buffalo	yonder	coming	his
ra	wakūru	ra	ūra	wē	riku	sa
have	sayings	walking	have	do	stand	coming

FREE TRANSLATION

Listen, he said, yonder the buffalo are coming,
These are his sayings, yonder the buffalo are coming,
They walk, they stand, they are coming,
Yonder the buffalo are coming.

Analysis.—This song is harmonic in structure and has a compass of 11 tones. The intervals are unusually large, only six being smaller than a fourth. It has been noted that the interval of a fourth appears to characterize songs associated with animals and with motion. This interval comprises 14 of the 25 progressions in this song. The final tone is preceded by a fourth lower, as in No. 2. A rhythmic unit occurs several times and the characteristic count division of the unit occurs in the opening portion of the song.

Long ago an old man named Nara'dudesa'ru had a dream and in his dream he saw a cloud of dust rolling along the ground. He sat and looked at the dust a long time until late in the afternoon. Then it looked like a crowd of people, but after the dust storm had passed he saw a great herd of buffalo.

No. 8. "The Waves of Dust"

(Catalogue No. 1113)

Recorded by WICITA BLAIN

Voice ♩ = 76
Drum ♩ = 120
Drum-rhythm similar to No. 2

Ha	tī	waka	īre	ra	waa [19]	kūra	ra
Listen	he	said	there	have do	coming	his	have

wakūru	īre	ra	waa	rū	tit	kahāru
sayings	there	have	coming	did	dust	earth

tīku		īre	ra	waa	rūte	rax
wave downward		there	have	coming	do	them

wīwari	hūsa
wallow	marked place

---

[19] This word signifies a great mass in motion.

Listen, he said,
There the buffalo are coming in a great herd,
These are his sayings,
There the buffalo are coming in a great herd,
The waves of dust roll downward,
There the buffalo are coming in a great herd,
They mark the place of the buffalo wallow.

Analysis.—This melody contains only the tones E flat, F and B flat, except G which occurs as next to the last note. This occurrence of G, however, makes possible the classification of the song as major in tonality. The song has a compass of 9 tones and its progressions consist of 28 whole tones and 7 larger intervals. The opening portion of the song suggests a chant and is followed by a rest. This is succeeded by a 3-measure phrase with a clear-cut rhythm and a descending trend of 9 tones. After a repetition of the rhythmic unit the song returns to the whole tone progressions on the highest tones of the compass. This phrase is followed by a second rhythmic unit. In several renditions the portions of the song resembling a chant were sung softly, the singer changing to a loud tone at the beginning of the rhythmic phrases. The drumbeat was in the same tempo throughout this song, differing from other ceremonial songs in which the drumbeat was rapid in the opening measures.

The next song is also concerning a dream of buffalo. The herd was scattered and a man was watching them. One of the buffalo lay down. The man wondered why the buffalo had lain down. That night he dreamed about the buffalo, who said that he had "taken pity" on the man. The buffalo promised the man that he would live to old age and be able to foretell events a long time before they came to pass.

Analysis.—This song is unusual in containing no interval of a whole tone. It contains 39 progressions, 12 of which are semitones and 11 are minor thirds. The transcription is from the first rendition, the tempo of the drum changing abruptly on the fourth measure as in certain other songs of this group. The tempo of the voice increased during the latter portion of the rendition and in the subsequent renditions. Such hastening of the tempo is not customary among Indians and was probably due to agitation on the part of the singer, who was totally blind. The rhythmic unit is not distinctive but occurred several times.

No. 9. "Unreal the Buffalo is Standing"

(Catalogue No. 1111)

Recorded by WICITA BLAIN

Voice ♩ = 76
Drum ♩ = 138 changing to ♩ = 76
Drum-rhythm similar to No. 2

Tĭ wa-ka a rā-ru te ra rĭ-kĭ kū-ra ra wa-kŭ-

ru e e e rā-ru te ra rĭ-ki i i i

tĭ wa-ka te ra rĭ-ki rā-ru te ra rĭ-ki i i

rā-ru te ra rĭ-ki i i rā-ru tex wa-rā-ru

kā-ri-ki e rā-a-ru tex ra a rĭ-ki tĭ wa-

ka a rā-ru te ra rĭ-ki kū-ra ra wa-kū-ru

rā-ru te ra rĭ-ki i i rā-ru te ra rĭ-ki i i

rā-ru tex warāru kā-ri-ki a rā-a-ru tex ra a rĭ-ki

| Tĭ | waka | rāru | te | ra | rĭki | kūra |
| He | said | not real | it | have | standing | his |

| ra | wakūru | rāru | te | ra | rĭki |
| have | sayings | not real | it | have | standing |

| rāru | tex | wa/raru | kāriki |
| not real | his | open space | standing |

FREE TRANSLATION

He said, unreal the buffalo is standing,
These are his sayings,
Unreal the buffalo is standing,
Unreal he stands in the open space,
Unreal he is standing.

LANCE DANCE

At a certain point in the Lance dance witnessed by the writer the decorated lances were carried around the lodge and the following song was sung. This constituted one of the most impressive portions of the ceremony. The song is very old and belonged to a woman who had two sons, the song being sung whenever they danced. The woman lived to be so old that she could not stand erect but she "was always singing this song while she was cooking or working." The words mean "Father, the band of the dead is coming." The woman who recorded the song was blind.

No. 10. "The Band of the Dead Is Coming"

(Catalogue No. 1091)

Recorded by EFFIE BLAIN

Voice ♩ = 63
Drum not recorded

Analysis.—Exactness in the repetition of an Indian song is shown in the renditions of this melody. Eight renditions were recorded without a break in the time except that the final tone was sometimes prolonged to the value of three quarter notes. In each rendition the song was sung twice. The connective phrase occurred between the second and third, and the fourth and fifth renditions. The song has a compass of nine tones, and progresses by whole tones except for three other intervals which occur only in downward progression.

BEAR DANCE

There was no opportunity to witness this dance, and its details were not made a subject of inquiry. Ten songs of the dance were recorded, the first five by a member of the Chaui Band and the last five by a member of the Skidi Band. These two groups of songs are strikingly different in musical character.

The next song was sung when all the participants in the Bear dance were seated. "Mother" was said to refer to the moon, and there was said to be a similar song containing the word "Father." A young man received this song in a dream, while mourning for his parents who had died. He saw a woman coming toward him, and said, "Mother is coming." The woman said," You have seen me, now you must learn this song." The young man learned the song, lived a long time afterwards, and took part in the Bear dance. When the song is used ceremonially there are six "stops" or verses, the general meaning of which is as follows:

1. "Mother is coming."
2. The young man, devotional by nature, imagines that he is still mourning for his parents.
3. "Mother stands yonder."
4. The young man says, "Mother, standing in the sky, I want you to take pity on me."
5. "Mother now ends" (stands still).
6. "I will now say, I mean the mother who alone stands forever in the sky" (the moon).

No. 11. "Mother is Coming"

(Catalogue No. 1117)

Recorded by WICITA BLAIN

Voice ♩ = 126
Drum ♩ = 138, changing to ♩ = 126
Drum-rhythm similar to No. 2

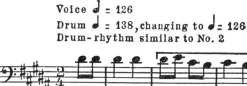

Analysis.—All the tones of the octave except the sixth and seventh occur in this song, which has a compass of 11 tones and is melodic in structure. It begins on next to the highest tone of the compass and ends on the lowest, which is the keynote. The rhythm is energetic and the phrases with continuously descending trend are somewhat unusual. The change in the tempo of the drum has been described in connection with other songs of this group.

In the next song we have an expression of the belief that a bear derives his "medicine power" from the sun and that the center of that power is in his palms. He stands facing the dawn in order that the first rays of the sun may strike his paws, upheld for the purpose. In this manner he renews his power from the sun. (Cf. Song 16.)

An old man named Lata′piü, long ago, fell asleep, and when he awoke he saw a strange sight. The sun was rising and a bear was pointing at the sunrise. The old man made this song about his vision and whenever he saw the sunrise he sang the song. Ever since that time the song has been used in the Bear dance.

No. 12. "The Bear is Pointing at the Sun"

(Catalogue No. 1119)

Recorded by WICITA BLAIN

Voice ♩ = 76
Drum ♩ = 132 Changing to ♩ = 76
Drum-rhythm similar to No. 2

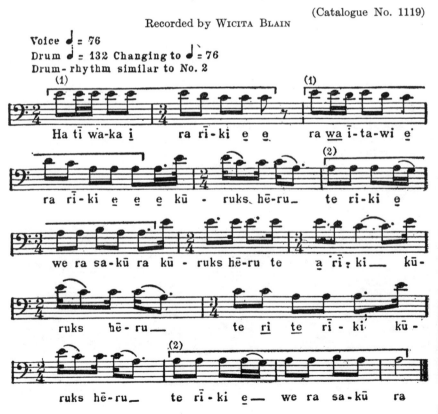

Ha	tī	waka	ra	rīki	ra	ītawi	ra	rīki .
Listen	he	said	have	stand	have	telling	have	stand

kŭruks	hĕru	te	rīki	we	ra
bear	yonder	it	stands	now	have

sakū	ra
sun	coming

FREE TRANSLATION

Listen, he said; he (the bear) stands,
I am telling this, yonder the bear stands,
It faces the east just before the sun appears,
Yonder the bear stands,
Now the sun is coming.

Analysis.—In this song we note the simplicity of rhythm which characterizes this entire group. A variety of progression occurs, though the major second comprises almost half the entire number of intervals. The song is minor in tonality, has a compass of six tones, and contains all the tones of the octave except the seventh. Two rhythmic units occur, the second reversing the count divisions of the first in its opening measure. The repetition of the first unit is not exact, as a third count is added to the first measure. The rhythm is particularly clear throughout the renditions. More than half the intervals are whole tones.

For a long time the Pawnee have called the cedar tree "mother," a custom which had its origin in the dream of a man who saw a cedar tree and thought it was "like a woman." He said, "This tree is made to look the same in winter and summer, and to stand up so nicely. The leaves of other trees fall but this tree is always green." This strange woman-tree made a noise like a bear and the song is used in the Bear dance.

Analysis.—This melody contains the tones of the second 5-toned scale and is characterized by a descending trend. The tempo of the drum begins to decrease in the fourth and fifth measures but the drum and voice do not fully coincide until the last part of the song. Minor thirds and major seconds comprise 23 of the 30 progressions, 5 of the remaining intervals being fourths. The song is melodic in structure and has a compass of 11 tones.

No. 13. "A Woman Stands Among the Trees"

(Catalogue No. 1118)

Recorded by Wicita Blain

Voice ♩ = 76 (♪ = 152)
Drum ♩ = 116 Changing to ♩ = 76
Drum-rhythm similar to No. 2

Tĭ	waka	tsapȧt	tĭ	re	karīkii	
He	said	woman	is	here	standing (among trees)	

we	rex	ra	ītawi	ēsi	ru	re
now	I	have	mentioning	loudly	does	she

karīkii	ra	tsiks	ta	rī	kake
standing	have	spirit	have	do	grunting

āhu
shouting

FREE TRANSLATION

He said, a woman is here standing among the trees,
Now I am telling it,
A woman is here standing among the trees,
Loudly does she stand among the trees,
From where her spirit dwells she grunts (like a bear).

Many years ago the Pawnee fought the Sioux, killing many. Among the Pawnee warriors was a man named Nada'kutade (Eagle Chief), father-in-law of the man who recorded the following song. Eagle Chief owned this song and sang it in the Bear dance. The fight with the Sioux was said to have taken place in a part of the country which was thickly wooded, the battle resulting in a victory for the Pawnee.

No. 14. "The Horse is Shouting"

(Catalogue No. 1120)

Recorded by WICITA BLAIN

Voice ♩ = 120
Drum ♩ = 138 Changing to ♩ = 120
Drum-rhythm similar to No. 2

Tī	waka	ra	wāka	ta	ā	ra	ītawi
He	said	have	shouting	going	on	have	telling

a	wē	ri	ku	ītawi	hū	a	kiriku	tix	rūta
about	now	it		mentioning	do	and	something	he	did

rā		waka		ta		ā		ra
have		shouting		going		on		have

a	we	rī	ku	ītawi	hū
about	now	it		mentioning	do

FREE TRANSLATION

He said, the horse is shouting,
I am telling it, the horse is shouting,
Now I am telling it,
The horse is shouting at something he did.

Analysis.—This song has a compass of only five tones and contains the tones of the minor triad and fourth.   In structure it is melodic.   The form of the melody is peculiar, the first seven measures containing the descent from E to A and the next two measures being framed on the descent from D to A.   This structure is repeated and the song closes with three measures on the descent from C to A. Only four intervals larger than a minor third occur in the song.   The gradual decrease in the tempo of the drum is similar to that in the song next preceding.

The singer said that when he was a young man living in Nebraska he saw a very old man who used a cane.   Even with this aid he could scarcely walk.   This old man had a dream in which he ascended a high hill and sat down.   The clouds were below him and he saw rain falling from the clouds; he also saw about 40 white horses and drove them; the white horses were probably the shapes assumed by the clouds in his dream.   The following song belonged to this old man but was not related to the foregoing dream.   It was sung in the Bear dance.

No. 15. "I Was Lost in the Timber"

(Catalogue No. 1121)

Recorded by WICITA BLAIN

Voice ♩ = 138
Drum ♩ = 144, changing to ♩ = 138
Drum-rhythm similar to No. 2

Ha	tī	waka	ra	tīra	ra	kū	ra
Listen	he	said	do	I come	do	did	have
ītawi	hīri	we	ra	tīra	tī	kuks
mentioning	place	now	do	I come	I	was
kahū	ra	hatsu
timber	have	lost

FREE TRANSLATION

Listen, he said, I come,
He told this to me,
I came to a place where I was lost in the timber,
I came to the place,
Now I come.

Analysis.—This song has a compass of five tones and contains only the tones of the minor triad and second. It is interesting to note that major thirds are more frequent than minor thirds, though the song is minor in tonality. Only one interval larger than a major third occurs in the melody. The time was broken between the renditions of this song.

The five remaining songs of the Bear dance were recorded by Dog Chief (pl. 1), whose father was one of the leading singers at the Bear dance in old times and who therefore has inherited the right to sing these songs.

No. 16. "I Am Like a Bear"

(Catalogue No. 1149)

Recorded by Dog Chief

Voice ♩ = 138
Drum not recorded

FREE TRANSLATION
I am like a bear,
I hold up my hands waiting for the sun to rise.

Analysis.—This song is harmonic in structure, the melody being based on the triad A flat–C–E flat, other tones occurring only as passing tones. The rhythmic interest lies in the 5–4 measures and in the fact that in two instances they alternate with 2–4, 3–4, and 4–4 measures in a somewhat irregular manner. The time was steadily maintained, the two renditions differing only in the time values of the first measure, which were changed to conform to the words of a second verse. The song is major in tonality but about 40 per cent of the intervals are minor thirds.

In describing the next song Dog Chief said that his father took part in the war against the Sioux and chased a member of that tribe who held a shield over his back as a protection. Dog Chief's father killed the Sioux and captured his horse, this song commemorating his deed of valor.

No. 17. Bear Dance Song (a)

(Catalogue No. 1153)

Recorded by Dog Chief

Analysis.—In this, as in other instances of very peculiar songs, the test of the song is in the ability of the singer to repeat it accurately. The several renditions of this song were uniform in every respect. The rhythm has a general effect of determination but contains no unit nor even a characteristic phrase. Twenty-five of the 41 intervals are whole tones. The interval of a seventh occurs six times and was sung with good intonation. The song contains only the tones D, F sharp, and G sharp and has a compass of 10 tones.

The words of the following song (not translated) state that Dog Chief took horns like those of a buffalo and put them on the horse he had captured.

No. 18. Bear Dance Song (b)

(Catalogue No. 1150)

Recorded by Dog Chief

Voice ♩ : 92
Drum not recorded

Analysis.—With the exception of two descending fifths and two descending fourths all the progressions in this song are whole tones and semitones. The first seven measures begin with the same tone, which is also the initial tone in five consecutive measures later in the song. This is next to the highest in the compass. A majority of the melody is on the tones C sharp, D sharp, and E, a few measures being on the tones G sharp and A. Thus the formation of the melody is seen to be based on intervals rather than on a scale or key. The rhythm is accurately repeated in the three renditions. The rhythmic unit is short and the rhythm of the song as a whole is "swung" by the triple measures occurring as measures 2, 9, 12, 18, and 19. It is interesting to note the irregular time spaces at which these triple measures occur. This shows that the rhythm of the entire song is an entity and offers a contrast to songs that consist of three or more distinct periods, each containing the same number of measures.

When the man returned with the horse he had captured, the people saw him running like a bear while the horse was galloping. This was commemorated in the following song.

No. 19. Bear Dance Song (c)

(Catalogue No. 1152)

Recorded by Dog Chief

Analysis.—This melody is peculiar in that about 40 per cent of its progressions are minor sixths or larger intervals. The intonation on these large intervals was fairly correct in all the renditions. The two most prominent tones are D and E, the former appearing as an accented tone in almost half the measures. Attention is directed to the descent of an octave which twice is accomplished in the space of a measure.

The words of the next song were said to mean "I am a brave man. I am acting like a bear." (The lack of a competent interpreter when Dog Chief's songs were recorded made it impossible to secure a more extended description and translation.)

No. 20. Bear Dance Song (d)

(Catalogue No. 1151)

Recorded by Dog Chief

Voice ♩ = 168
Drum not recorded

Analysis.—This song is clearly harmonic in feeling, though three measures in the latter part of the song begin with nonharmonic tones. It has a compass of 12 tones and is based on the fourth 5-toned scale. Progression is chiefly by major and minor thirds. Two rhythmic units occur, and a comparison of these units forms the principal interest of the rhythm. Rests occur at the end of each phrase and after a detached tone in the fifth measure. These rests were clearly given in both renditions of the song.

SONGS OF THE DEER SOCIETY

The Wichita Indians are said to have originated this society, which has been discontinued for many years. The dance of the society was held in the autumn when the corn was ripe, and its purpose was "to find out whether a man would be killed when going on the warpath." The dances took place in an earth lodge. A custom of the society, described by James R. Murie, appears to have been a testing of the powers of its members. Mr. Murie said, "These men drank mescal, putting about half a bean in a kettle of water. After drinking it they fell unconscious. An attendant then ran the jaw of a garfish along the man's spine and if he recovered consciousness he was not considered fitted to belong to the society. Members of this society had power over snakes and their dance was allied to that of the Mokis. Each dancer carried a fox skin and held in his mouth a plain bone or reed whistle on which he blew as he danced." There were four singers, each carrying a bow in one hand and a gourd rattle in the other.

Two songs of the society were recorded by Mark Evarts (pl. 2, *b*), who said that his father was one of its dancers. He said that the ceremony of the Deer Society lasted four days and nights and that this song was sung just before daylight.

No. 21. "How Near is the Morning?"

(Catalogue No. 1159)

Recorded by MARK EVARTS

FREE TRANSLATION

Part 1

The chief speaks to his attendant, saying, "Go out and see how the stars stand. Tell us how near is the morning."
The attendant returns and says, "It is almost morning."
The chief says to the dancers, "Wake up, men. It is almost morning."

Part 2

The chief speaks to his attendant. saying, "Go out and see how the stars stand. Tell us how near is the morning."
The attendant returns and says, "The morning star is coming up."
The chief says to the singers, "Change the song. The morning star is rising."

Analysis.—This song consists of two parts, each containing nine measures and ending with the same phrase. This phrase, together with the accented subdominant at the beginning of the second half of the song, gives a plaintive character to the melody. The progressions of the opening measures suggest an inquiry and are marked by consecutive whole tones on the upper tones of the compass. Two rhythmic units occur, the second being an extension of the first. Progression is by a variety of intervals but the major second comprises about three-fifths of the entire number.

The use of the following song was not explained.

No. 22. "Spring is Opening"

(Catalogue No. 1160)

Recorded by MARK EVARTS

Voice ♩ = 104
Drum not recorded

FREE TRANSLATION

Spring is opening,
I can smell the different perfumes of the white weeds used in the dance.

Analysis.—This song is based on the fourth 5-toned scale and has a compass of 12 tones. About two-thirds of the progressions are downward. This proportion of descending intervals is not uncommon in Indian songs, but this melody contains, in several instances, a succession of four descending progressions, which is unusual. Almost the entire song consists of repetitions of the rhythmic unit.

SONG OF THE WHITE LANCE SOCIETY

The ceremony and dance of this society were witnessed by Mrs. Blain when a child, the ceremony being called Naristaka (*naris,* ceremony; *taka,* white). She stated that the men taking part in the dance had half their bodies painted red and half black, and their position in dancing was such that the side of their bodies painted red was toward the sunrise and that painted black was toward the sunset. Each man held the hands of the men on either side of him, and it was required that they keep hold of each other's hands during the entire dance. "Thus if they came to a tree as they danced they could not loose their hands but must stand there and dance."

The general idea of the next song is that it is better to die bravely when young than to live to an enfeebled old age. In this, as in other Pawnee war songs, we see a light estimate upon the value of life as compared to success in war. The song belonged originally to a brave man who lived to an advanced age. When this was sung in a dance he rose and told the young men that it was a painful thing to live to be so old. The song was also sung by men in a battle, this being the last song they sang "when they were all tired out and so nearly beaten that even their hair was disheveled." It was further stated that "sometimes when men were having this dance an enemy attacked the village. This was the song they sang as they drove the enemy away." The song was also used in the scalp dances that followed the return of a successful war party.

No. 23. "Old Age is Painful"

Recorded by EFFIE BLAIN

(Catalogue No. 1078)

Voice ♩ = 66
Drum not recorded

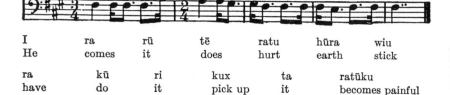

I	ra	rū	tē	ratu	hūra	wiu
He	comes	it	does	hurt	earth	stick

ra	kū	ri	kux	ta	ratūku
have	do	it	pick up	it	becomes painful

FREE TRANSLATION

He comes.
It hurts to use a cane.
It becomes painful to pick it up.

Analysis.—Four renditions were recorded. The first and second renditions were interrupted by the shrill cries given by women in a war dance, the interruptions occurring in the eighth measure of the first and the ninth measure of the second rendition. After the second rendition the singer spoke several sentences rapidly and after the third rendition she repeated the shrill cries. The third and fourth renditions were sung without interruption. The foregoing is an interesting example of the performance of this class of songs. The tempo is slow and the melody is marked by a steadily descending trend. The song is harmonic in structure, contains all the tones of the octave, and has a compass of 11 tones.

SONGS OF THE RAVEN LANCE SOCIETY

The custom of the Pawnee concerning the raven lance (*kakutsaa*) was similar to that of the Mandan.[20]   A warrior who carried this lance into battle and planted it in the ground was obliged to defend its position with his life. If he were killed, his comrades brought back the lance. By the Pawnee informant the lance was described as a staff wrapped with otter hide and having a crook at the upper end. It was decorated with eagle feathers and bore the body of a raven, commonly designated as a crow.

The dance of the Raven Lance Society was said to be "almost like that in which the dancers painted half their bodies red and half black," referring to the White Lance Society. The original owner of this dance lived to extreme old age and, as he had no children, he gave the dance to a young man who was one of his nearest relatives. One day the people said, "Some Indians are coming to attack us." The young man who had received the dance took his raven lance, mounted his pony, and went to get the old man. They rode together on the pony to a place near the fight and then went forward on foot, but the old man could not go as fast as the warriors. The old man called, "I am still coming," and the young man came back and helped him forward. The aged man was proud to see that the young man to whom he had given his dance was among the leaders in the fight. The enemy shot and killed the young man, and the lance was brought back with his body. Then the old man sang this song. In the manner of recording the song there was a wailing which was said to be "the old man crying because the young man had been killed and he had no more relatives," yet he loved the lance and all that it symbolized. He died soon afterwards and, as he was too old to give the dance to anyone else, the Pawnee do not have the dance at the present time.

---

[20] Cf. Mandan and Hidatsa Music, pp. 48 and 49, including "Song to the Raven"; also Lowie, Societies of the Mandan and Hidatsa Indians, pp. 313-314.

No. 24. "Beloved Emblem"

(Catalogue No. 1133)

Recorded by JOHN LUWAK

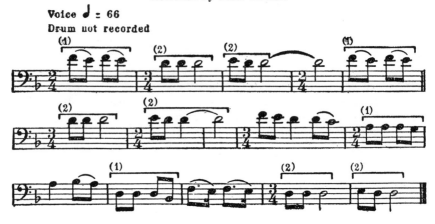

FREE TRANSLATION

(An exclamation of endearment)
Beloved emblem, they are carrying it forward,
Beloved emblem, they are bringing it back.

Analysis.—This is a plaintive melody with a compass of 12 tones. The first tone is the highest in the compass and the trend of the melody is steadily downward to the final tone, which is the lowest in the compass. If this song were transcribed in accordance with the pitch of the phonograph record it would have a signature of six sharps. For convenience of observation it is presented with a signature of one flat, changing the key from D sharp minor to D minor. Songs with a similar change of signature are Nos. 29, 30, 36, 39, 51, 52, 62, and 85.

The next song belonged to the singer's father and was his war song.

Analysis.—This song has a compass of 12 tones and contains all the tones of the octave. The third occurs only twice, both occurrences being as short unaccented tones in the first half of the song. The intervals which characterize the song are the major second as an interval of progression and the fourth and fifth as portions of the framework of the melody. Thus the first six measures are based on the descending fifth C to F, followed by B flat to F; the next four measures are on the descending fifth G to C, and the song closes with the intervals C to F and B flat to F in the lower octave. The major second constitutes about 83 per cent of the entire number of intervals. The tempo was well sustained but the intonation was not steady. Six renditions were recorded with no break in the time except between the second and third when a sentence was spoken rapidly. It is in accordance with Indian custom to interject rapid sentences between renditions of a war song, or even to interrupt a song with spoken words, the subject being that of the song.

No. 25. Crow Lance Society Song

(Catalogue No. 1083)

Recorded by EFFIE BLAIN

Voice ♩ = 84
Drum not recorded

FREE TRANSLATION

If I did anything great in battle I would be a crow (member of the Crow Society).

SONGS OF THE KITSITA SOCIETY

The identity of this society is not fully established. Those taking part in the dance were painted as in the White Lance Society and "held their lives in such light esteem as to be called unreal." In describing this song the singer said that long ago there was a woman who had only one child, a boy, who grew up to be a handsome young man. The first dance he saw was that of the Kitsita and he said to his mother, "I like that dance; I wish I could be in it." His mother said, "No, my son, the dancers are acting like certain animals that have only a short time to live and that is why I do not want you to dance with them."

Analysis.—Two rhythmic units occur in this song, their repetitions comprising the entire melody. The first rhythmic unit is transcribed in a 5-count measure as the secondary accent varies, in some instances the third, and in others the fourth count of the group being slightly accented. In some renditions the tempo is slightly hastened at the opening of the second rhythmic unit. This song contains a larger variety of intervals than a majority of the Indian songs which have been analyzed, although more than half the progressions are whole tones.

No. 26. "The Lance Dancers"

(Catalogue No. 1124)

Recorded by JOHN LUWAK

Drum-rhythm

Ru	īra	rax	ru	rīwi	tsapåt	tī	waku
There	them	have	there	walking	woman	she	said

ku	kakī	ra	riks	kītsita	rax
there	no	have	not real	lance dancers	them

ru	rīwi
there	walking

FREE TRANSLATION

There they are walking, a woman said,
You see them but they are not real,
They are the Lance dancers.

An informant said that the song next following was sung "when men made up their minds that it was no matter if they were killed." The tradition concerning this song was related by the singer as follows: The Pawnee were on the buffalo hunt and were climbing a hill in search of the herd. One family had a little boy with them and while they were climbing the hill another tribe overtook them and killed the little boy's father. When the Pawnee had run away from the other tribe they began to kill buffalo. The little boy was very happy about the hunt, not realizing that his father was dead. The child's mother wept and said, "Little boy, you are glad because they are killing buffalo but your father is dead and there is no one to bring us meat as he used to do." She sang this song, the words being those that she had spoken to the little boy.

No. 27. Lance Dance Song (a)

(Catalogue No. 1081)

Recorded by EFFIE BLAIN

Voice ♩ = 56
Drum not recorded

Analysis.—This song, like No. 23, was interrupted by shrill cries. In the second rendition these cries were given at the beginning of the fifth measure. Afterwards the singer resumed the tempo and rhythm of the song. Such cries were also given between the third and fourth renditions. The song has a compass of 12 tones and progresses only by whole tones and major and minor thirds.

The next song was composed by a man who dreamed that he "heard some one crying and singing at the same time."

Analysis.—This melody is minor in tonality and is characterized by an effect of deep sadness. The two rhythmic units differ only in the division of the last count. Attention is directed to the change of accent in the seventh measure, the final tone of the rhythmic unit falling on an accented instead of an unaccented count. This change represents the break in rhythm which frequently occurs just after the middle of an Indian song. The signature of the key of B is used in the transcription of this melody, although the third above that tone does not occur. The song is classified as lacking the third.

Except for an ascending fourth the song progresses entirely by major seconds and minor thirds.

No. 28. Lance Dance Song (b)

(Catalogue No. 1093)

Recorded by EFFIE BLAIN

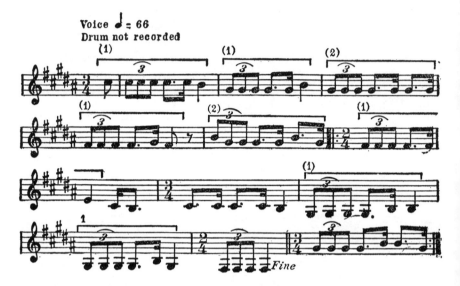

SONGS OF THE WOLF SOCIETY

Only two songs of this society were obtained. It was the custom of the Wolf Society to pound on a tanned buffalo hide, instead of a drum, during their songs. The first song of this society was said to "go back to the time when the Pawnee lived in Nebraska where the white or silver fox was commonly found." The animal was also designated as a kit fox by James R. Murie. Tradition states that a war party found a white fox singing this song.[21]

Analysis.—The distinction between the tones transcribed as A natural and A flat was clearly given in all the renditions and the song is classified as both major and minor in tonality. The song is unusual in its initial progression of an octave and in its compass of two octaves, the lowest tones being sung with clearness. About two-thirds of the progressions are whole and half tones, the latter producing a peculiar wailing effect.

---

[21] Cf. Teton Sioux Music, p. 183, in which a man is taught a song by a wolf. The same work relates instances in which wolves appeared to warriors.

No. 29. "The White Fox"

(Catalogue No. 1103)

Recorded by WICITA BLAIN

Voice ♩ = 69
Drum not recorded

A— Ha ī ra he i ya ha ī ra— ha ī ra he— i ya— a i ya i— a he tī re ka-hū-ra rā wa he he— ho i-rā-ri tī wa-ku ī-sa ka-hū-ra i kī-wa-ku re ka-hū - rā ra wa a

Ha	ī	ra	tī	re	kahūra		rā
Yonder	it	comes	this	then	the expanse of earth		has

wa	irāri	tī	waku	īsa	kahūra
width	my brother	he	spoke	behold	the expanse

kīwaku		re	kahūra		rā		wa
the white foxes		they	the expanse of earth		has		width

FREE TRANSLATION

Yonder it comes.
The expanse of earth is wide,
My brother the fox spoke and said,
"Behold and see the wideness of the earth,
The white foxes know the earth is wide."

The second Wolf Society song was said to belong to an old man who lived many years ago. In explanation it was said, "Before the people had horses they traveled on foot and often became tired out from walking." The old man to whom this song belonged said "Tirawa gave us this land to walk upon and he gave us the light. I can see my way, but I am so tired that I can go no farther." According to Mr. Murie this song might be sung in reference to any unfortunate circumstance or occurrence.   Another song of the days before the Pawnee obtained horses is No. 78, entitled "You Need not Fear the Horse."

No. 30. "It Is Mine, This Country Wide"

(Catalogue No. 1106)

Recorded by WICITA BLAIN

Ha	ī	ra	ha	tā	tīri	rūra	rāwa
Yonder	there	coming	yonder	I	mine	land	wide

pits	ka	sīratu	rūti	kux	rūra	
hateful	consider	hurtful	did	my	land	

ra	wī	ta	tīri	rūra	rāwa
strangely	became	I	mine	land	wide

FREE TRANSLATION

Yonder they are coming,
Although strange misfortunes have befallen me,
Yet it is mine, this country wide.

Analysis.—This song, like the song next preceding, has the unusual compass of two octaves.   It is harmonic in structure and contains the tones of the fourth 5-toned scale.   No rhythmic unit occurs in the song, which progresses by an unusual variety of intervals.   The fifth occurs six times, which is an unusual prominence of that interval.

WAR SONGS

Three classes of war songs are here presented and comprise a song concerning a conquered warrior of the Cheyenne Tribe, several songs of Pawnee warriors, and songs which were sung at two gatherings of the tribe attended by the writer, these gatherings being in honor of Pawnee soldiers who had recently returned from the World War.

The first song commemorates a well-known event in Pawnee history. About the year 1852 the Cheyenne and Arapaho returned from Washington, where they had gone to make a treaty with the Government of the United States. Among them was a Cheyenne of great reputation named Touching Cloud, who, because of the incident to be related, was afterwards known among the Pawnee as Iron Shirt. This man had in his employ a Mexican who could cut round disks from the thin frying pans used at that time. Touching Cloud had these disks sewed on a shirt and cap, the pieces overlapping as in old-world armor. Soon after the return of the treaty party, the Cheyenne attacked the Pawnee, who were hunting buffalo. Touching Cloud felt so secure that he rode directly among the Pawnee. His arms were so stiffened by the metal disks on his sleeves that he could use no weapon except a sword but he used this so effectively that he and his party drove the Pawnee back to their village. The Pawnee were unable to explain the fearlessness of this man and talked of it among themselves. In the village was a young man named Carrying-the-shield who had not gone with the hunters. He listened to what they said and remembered something told him by his father, who was keeper of a sacred bundle. His father had four sons and gave them four sacred arrows, each a different color. The arrow received by Carrying-the-shield was red. In giving the arrow his father said, "Use this arrow when you are in great danger and it will save your life." So Carrying-the-shield took the arrow and a bow, went out and met a party of Pawnee retreating with the Cheyenne in pursuit. The retreating party opened and let him through. Touching Cloud made ready to attack him but the youth shot him in the eye with the red arrow and he fell from his horse. The Pawnee "counted coup" on his body and found that he wore, concealed beneath his outer raiment, the metal-covered shirt made for him by the Mexican. Therefore he was known as Iron Shirt among the Pawnee.

Analysis.—An ascending tenth occurs in this song, representing an ascent from the lowest to almost the highest tone of the compass. The rhythmic unit is interesting and of frequent occurrence. The song is major in tonality and the most frequent interval is a major third.

No. 31. Song Concerning Iron Shirt

(Catalogue No. 1108)

Recorded by WICITA BLAIN

Voice ♩ = 108
Drum ♩ = 126
Drum rhythm similar to No. 26

Wē	ra	tsa	papitsīsu	ruks	tax
Now	yonder	lie	metal	did	have

kāsiu	ra	rūte	rakū	ru
shirt on	have	is	sitting, put one side	have

tsiks	ta	isti	ra	papitsīsu
him	have	protection	have	metal

ruks	tax	kāsiu
did	have	shirt on

FREE TRANSLATION

Now he lies yonder.
He who has on a metal shirt.
The protection in which he trusted is set aside.

Three generations of Pawnee chiefs bore the name of Eagle Shield and the song next following was said to have belonged to the chief of the first generation. The day after he returned from a war expedition he mounted his best horse and rode around the camp singing this song. The words mean "I wonder how long I am to live in this world." In explanation it was said the old warrior was wondering what his fate might be when he again took the warpath.

Analysis.—This song comprises four periods, the rhythmic unit occurring in the first three while the last period opens with the same count division as the rhythmic unit but changes to a succession of eighth notes. No change of measure length occurs in the song.

Drum and voice are in the same tempo and coincide on the first of each count.   Three renditions were recorded and show no points of difference.

No. 32. Eagle Chief's War Song

(Catalogue No. 1128)

Recorded by JOHN LUWAK

Voice ♩ = 66
Drum ♩ = 66
Drum-rhythm similar to No. 2

A certain young man was afraid of the storm and wept when he heard the thunder, but in a dream the thunder spoke to him slowly and said, "Do not be afraid, your father is coming."   He heard the thunder sing the following song, learned it, and sang it when he went to war.   His name was Eagle and he lived to be one of the old warriors of the tribe.

No. 33. "The Thunder Spoke Quietly"

(Catalogue No. 1086)

Recorded by EFFIE BLAIN

Voice ♩ = 63
Drum not recorded

(1)   (1)

A - hē - ru   i   ra' - u   a - hē - ru   i   ra - u

2

a __ ti ra ha - he   a   (2) he   pā - hi - tu ra ti

wa - ku   ti ra ki - ri - ru   a __ ti ra hā - he   e

Ahēru	i	raŭ	a	tī	ra	harāhe [22]	pāhitu
Dear	it	that is	and	this	have	good	quietly
ra	tī	waku	tī	ra	kirīru	a	tī
have	him	saying	this	have	thundering	and	this
ra	hārahe						
have	good						

---

[22] The second syllable of this word was omitted by the singer.

Beloved, it is good,
He is saying quietly,
The thunder, it is good.

Analysis.—The tempo of this song was slightly *rubato*, but the accents were clearly given. A portion of the song lies above the fundamental tone and a portion below it, which is somewhat unusual in Pawnee songs, although occurring frequently in the songs of certain other tribes. Progression is by a wide variety of intervals, one-third of which are intervals of a fourth. The song is minor in tonality and contains only the tones of the minor triad and second.

In explanation of the following song it was said that long ago there was a society called *Iruska Virau* (or *Pirau*), translated "children of the Iruska." Members of this society did everything contrariwise. Thus in a fight they would not fire at the enemy unless commanded *not* to do so.[23] The song next following was said to be a song of that society and was recorded by the chief of the Chaui Band. The same melody with different words was used by the Skidi Band, the words of their version stating that a young man was told in a dream that he would be killed the next day, but felt no fear. John Luwak (pl. 2, *a*), who recorded the song, said it was his own war-dance song, explaining the words as follows: "A dead person wanted a certain warrior to do right, so he said to him, 'If anyone is kind-hearted and good to the poor he is made a chief and has a great name. When he dies we in the spirit land are glad and want to go and meet him because he was kind and good.'"

Analysis.—Attention is directed to the rhythmic form of this song and a comparison of the rhythmic units. The song opens with a rather long phrase, which is repeated. The following tones represent a repetition of the rhythmic unit, but a second unit is introduced and continues to the end of the song. This is shorter and livelier than the first, though bearing some resemblance to it. The song is harmonic in structure and contains the tones of the second 5-toned scale. Only three intervals occur which are larger than a minor third. The tempo of the drum is slightly faster than that of the voice, this appearing in all renditions of the song.

---

[23] Cf.Teton Sioux Music, p. 157, concerning the Heyoka Kaga (Fool impersonation).

No. 34. "He Comes"

(Catalogue No. 1125)

Recorded by JOHN LUWAK

Voice ♩ = 84
Drum ♩ = 100
Drum-Rhythm similar to No. 26

A - a̱ - hē - ru — ra - a   hē - e̱ - ru — ra—

hē - e̱ - ru   ra - a   hē - ru — ra - a   hē - e̱ - ru — ra—

hē - e̱ - ru   a̱ a̱   hē - ru — ra—   hē - e̱ - ru   ra - a

a̱   kī-i̱ - tu — tix   wa̱ wä-ke   he̱ e̱   wē-e̱ - ta   a̱   ax-

a̱ - a̱ - ra͡u   i - sī - rit — rä   a̱   ta-we

Ahēru	raa	hēru	kītu	tix	wāke
Dear	come	dear	all	them	spoke
he	wēta	axra͡u	isīrit	rä	tawe
here	is coming	he is	openly	have	amongst

FREE TRANSLATION

Beloved, come beloved, all of them spoke,
All of them spoke,
It is openly known that he did these things.

49716°—29——6

A woman's pleasure at the return of victorious warriors is expressed in the following song which was sung at the Scalp dances. Among the Pawnee, as in other tribes, the scalps of slain warriors were carried in the victory dance.

No. 35. "A Woman Welcomes the Warriors"

(Catalogue No. 1104)

Recorded by WICITA BLAIN

Hia			we	ta	tū	ra	kerit
A woman's exclamation of surprise			now	I	you	have	seen

TRANSLATION

Ah, now I have seen you.

Analysis.—This song contains two phrases designated as rhythmic units, each of which comprises three measures. The first phrase consists entirely of descending intervals and has a compass of an octave. The second phrase begins with the same count division as the first and comprises almost three measures, but it differs from the first phrase in containing one ascending interval and having a compass of only six tones. These rhythmic phrases were accurately given in all the renditions. The melody tones are those of the fourth 5-toned scale.

Two dances of historic interest to the Pawnee were held in honor of members of the tribe who had served in the World War. These dances were held on June 6 and 7, 1919, and were attended by the writer. The place of the gatherings was a large wooden structure, north of Pawnee and located among the members of the Skidi Band. (Pl. 7, *c*.) It was six-sided, with a dirt floor, and had an entrance toward the east which resembled the covered entrance to the earth lodge.

The first gathering was attended by about 200 Indians and the building was closely packed at the second gathering, those unable to gain admission being crowded around the windows and door.

The Pawnee Tribe was represented in the United States Army by 40 young men, all except one of whom returned in full health and vigor. One of the Pawnee soldiers died from disease in France. None were wounded, although many saw hard service at the front. Several were with the Rainbow Division, and on one occasion when there was a call for volunteers for dangerous service four Pawnee stepped forward and were accepted. One of these men brought back a German helmet as a trophy and his mother carried it in the victory dance as a scalp was carried in former times. The helmet was fastened to a pole at the top of which a captured knife was fastened like the point of a lance. A Pawnee said: "While the boys were away we prayed for their safe return. We did this at every public gathering and it looks as though our prayers had been answered."

The dance on June 6 was the rejoicing of the tribe and that on the day following was more formal, being attended by many white persons from the town of Pawnee. At the first dance the soldiers were honored by their families and friends, especially by the women, about 45 of whom were in the circle. It was a time of general rejoicing, sometimes three persons being on their feet at the same time, singing, narrating some incident, or giving a gift. Old war songs were sung with new words appropriate to the occasion. For example, one man had composed words which mentioned airplanes and submarines, these words being sung to an old tune. A woman had composed two similar songs, and, crossing the circle, she stood in front of the chief (James R. Murie) and sang them alone, without the drum. Throughout the entire afternoon there were frequent repetitions of the shrill, quavering cry with which the Indian women express pleasure or approval.

Two of the most interesting songs heard on this occasion had their origin in two dreams by John Luwak. The melody of the two was the same, but the words referred to different dreams. Luwak, who speaks no English, said that his friends translated to him the newspaper accounts of the war and that he "felt badly that our boys must cross the ocean and suffer so much." So he prayed daily to Tirawa, saying, "Help our boys over there, so they will all come back strong and let me live to see them again." One night he fell asleep, after such a prayer, and "in his sleep someone told him that it would not be long before he would see the Pawnee boys again." He dreamed, and in his dream he saw thousands of white people and heard them sing this song. They were very happy and were dancing and waving flags; even the oldest people were dancing.

He had never seen white people behave in this manner, and it surprised him greatly. A few days later he heard of the signing of the armistice and the scenes of its celebration. The next night he dreamed again, and in his dream he saw a circle of Indians dancing and heard them sing the same melody. In the middle of the dance circle was a tall pole, and on top of it was a skull. Two white women stood near him watching the dance, and one of them pointed to the skull, saying, "Look, I wonder what that can be." When he awoke he thought perhaps the skull indicated that many of the enemy had been killed but later he interpreted the skull as representing a helmet. As already mentioned, a helmet was carried in the victory dance.

Soon after these dreams there was a gathering of the Pawnee at the earth lodge and Luwak rose, told his dreams, and sang the song, which was readily learned by the people and sung at subsequent gatherings prior to the return of the soldiers. The words heard in his first dream are those presented with the transcription. The words with his second dream were addressed to the skull: "At this, whoever you may have belonged to, you are now hung on a pole." The words of the song when sung at the victory dance were connected with events of the recent war.

No. 36. Song for Returned Pawnee Soldiers

(Catalogue No. 1134)

Recorded by JOHN LUWAK

Voice ♩ = 76
Drum ♩ = 76
Drum rhythm similar to No. 2

FREE TRANSLATION

You are coming.
You are the ones for whom I am looking

Analysis.—The frequency of the fourth characterizes this song, which contains only the tones of the major triad and fourth. It is a vigorous melody, progressing freely within its compass of an octave.

The dance on the second day (June 7) was opened ceremonially, a pipe being lighted with a coal from the central fire and smoked by the chief and the men seated near him. Many gifts were bestowed upon the returned soldiers, among these gifts being two white horses

led into the dance lodge by women.   Some of the young men were in
the full costume of Indian warriors, others were in civilian clothing,
and Lawrence Murie wore the khaki uniform in which he had served
with the artillery at the front.   The young soldier who directed the
dancing carried a sword which had belonged to one of his ancestors.
The principal dance was the grass dance, followed by the war dance.
The former is common to all the tribes of the northern plains, extending even to the Kutenai.   According to Miss Fletcher, the dance
originally was connected with the Hethushka Society of the Omaha,
a society whose object was "to stimulate an heroic spirit among the
people and to keep alive the memory of historic and valorous acts." [24]

A touching event in the second day's gathering was the expression
of sympathy for the parents of the young man who died in France.
They stood before the assembly while the chief and other leading
men talked to them.   The speaker placed his hands on the man's
head, drawing them down the man's arms to his hands; he also held
the man's hands closely in his own as he talked to him in a tender,
earnest manner.

Numerous speeches were made, and the occasion was marked by
dignity as well as rejoicing.   The young soldiers appeared to be in
excellent health, were friendly toward all, and made a good impression
upon the white people who attended the gathering.

The song next following was sung by the women on the second day
of the victory dance.   It is an "honor song" and belonged to an old
man named Brown Bear (*guruks*, bear; *narahata*, brown), who died
not long ago.   At a war dance he used to rise and sing this song
without the drum, and "when he sang everybody cried."   The
custom of weeping and even wailing aloud at public gatherings has
not been noted in tribes previously studied.   The words of the song
meant, "Nobody knows when the world will end."   The informant
added, "The old man used to say 'there is one person who knows
when the world will end.' "

Analysis.—This is one of the "crying songs," and the sliding tone,
especially in measures 7, 8, 13, and 14, is impossible to transcribe.
The time was well maintained throughout the song.   Attention is
directed to a comparison of the count-divisions in the two rhythmic
units and in the fifth and sixth measures from the close of the song.
All the tones of the octave occur in the melody which progresses by a
wide variety of intervals.

[24] Fletcher and La Flesche, The Omaha Tribe, Twenty-seventh Ann. Rept. Bur. Amer. Ethn., p. 459.

No. 37. Brown Bear's Song

(Catalogue No. 1085)

Recorded by EFFIE BLAI

Voice ♩ = 69
Drum not recorded

The next song was also sung by the women at the victory dance and was said to be "in the style of the Lance dance songs." It is a woman's song and would be sung by a woman whose husband or son was on the warpath. She would also sing it at the dance held after their return. The words mean, "They are coming yonder, the men who belong to the Lance Society (*Tirupa*)." Among the other songs used at this time was one which belonged to Roaming Chief and appears as No. 67 in the present work.

No. 38. Women's War Song

(Catalogue No. 1082)

Recorded by EFFIE BLAIN

Voice ♩ = 63 (♪ = 126)
Drum not recorded

a, Miniature group of Pawnee Thunder ceremony exhibited in Field Museum of Natural History

b, Framework (probably sweat lodge) near ceremonial earth lodge

c, Structure in which victory dances and hand games were held

COSTUMES

a, War leader; *b*, bear medicine man; *c*, woman's Ghost dance dress; *d*, dancer wearing "crow" dance bustle.
Exhibited in Field Museum of Natural History

Analysis.—Four renditions of this song were recorded without a break in the time. This is interesting because of the 7–8 measures which were always sung in correct time. The transcription is from the first rendition. The only differences were that in the later renditions the seventh measure was omitted and the first tone in the next to the last measure was sung as C instead of E. Such differences are slight but are important to observe in a study of Indian music. The keynote is more prominent in this song than in a majority of the songs under analysis, this tone occurring in every measure except the first. Nine of the 32 intervals are fourths, which is an unusually large proportion of this interval. The melody tones are those of the second 5-toned scale. A downward sliding of the voice, impossible to transcribe, occurred at the end of the first and third measures.

HAND GAME SONGS

On two occasions the writer had the privilege of attending a hand game of the Pawnee held in the same lodge where the victory dances for returned soldiers had been held. (Pl. 7, *c*.) The first of these games was in 1919 and the second in the following year. The number of Indians in attendance was more than 200. In former times this game was played only by men and the objects hidden were short sticks, but at the present time both men and women take part in the game, hiding small balls, slightly larger than bullets. The man holding the balls moves his hands above his head, puts them behind his back, and does everything possible to mystify and confuse his opponent, while the songs grow more excited as the moment for making the guess approaches. Ghost dance songs are sung in the dancing which takes place at intervals during the game. The balls are hidden by players of one side until the opponents have made five correct guesses in succession.

The games are often of long duration, the first game attended by the writer continuing about six hours. This game was opened in a ceremonial manner by James R. Murie, chief of the Skidi Band, who also recorded the guesses by means of decorated sticks. Seven feathered sticks were placed upright in the ground before him, [25] and this was said to be "as in the Ghost dance." [26] The woman who "gave the dance" stood in the center of the lodge and appointed

[25] Two sets of such sticks are illustrated by Culin, each set consisting of eight sticks. In one set these are 17 inches long, four painted yellow and four painted blue, and all feathered like arrows. In the other set each stick bears a little hoop at its end, decorated with feathers. The same authority illustrates a set of four hiding sticks, 1¾ inches long, marked in pairs alike, one pair with six notches on one side and one notch on the other side, and the other pair with an incised cross on each side of the sticks. (Culin, Stewart, Games of the North American Indians, Twenty-fourth Ann. Rept. Bur. Amer. Ethn., pp. 274, 275, Washington, 1907.)

[26] The number seven is particularly sacred in the Ghost dance. Thus there were seven Ghost dance leaders, wearing sacred crow feathers as emblems of their leadership.

those who should lead the two opposing sides. These in turn selected those who should hide the balls. It was customary to give the balls to persons sitting next each other, the guesser indicating by a gesture whether he (or she) believed the balls to be in the two outer hands, the two inner, or one outer and one inner hand. The writer was invited to sit beside a member of the tribe and join in the game, attempting to hide the balls in the manner of the Indians.

An unfortunate though not unusual circumstance took place in the dances which occurred during this game. The woman who gave the hand game was afflicted with what was termed a "Ghost dance fit." [27] She staggered and moaned in a pitiful manner but did not fall to the ground. Several persons went to her aid and restored her in the manner peculiar to the Ghost dance.[28]

The second hand game attended by the writer took place on April 16, 1921, and was given by Mrs. Good Eagle (pl. 2, c), who recorded Song No. 80. This was said to be her hand game, not only because she gave the invitations and provided the feast, but because certain features of the game, as played that day, had been revealed to her in a dream. The symbolism of certain articles used in that game was not made known to the singers and perhaps is known only to herself. The game was held in the same 6-sided lodge as the former hand game and the victory dances. (Pl. 7, c.) As on the former occasion, Mr. Murie opened the game in a ceremonial manner. The doors were closed and a filled pipe was offered to the earth and the sky. Mrs. Good Eagle was a dignified hostess, standing in the center of the lodge and appointing those who should lead the two sides of players. After the game the doors were again closed and a tiny portion of each sort of food was ceremonially offered and then laid beside the fire space, opposite the door. A bountiful feast was then served. According to Indian custom, each person provided his own utensils and the food was served in large containers. The writer shared in the feast.

Eight of the songs used at this game, during the hiding of the balls, were later recorded by Horse Chief, a prominent singer at the drum. In some of these songs there were no words and in others the words are obsolete, the singer repeating them but having no knowledge of their meaning.

---

[27] The woman undoubtedly suffered from the early stages of what, in the Ghost dance, would have been a trance. Mooney states that he "was able to note all the stages of the phenomenon . . . through the staggering, the rigidity, the unconsciousness, and back again to wakefulness. On two occasions my partner in the dance, each time a woman, came under the influence and I was thus enabled to note the very first nervous tremor of her hand and mark it as it increased in violence until she broke away and staggered toward the medicine man within the circle. Young women are usually the first to be affected, then older women, and lastly men." (Mooney, James, The Ghost Dance Religion, Fourteenth Ann. Rept. Bur. Ethn., pt. 2, p. 923, Washington, 1896.)

[28] The "Shaker religion" has been introduced among the Indians at Neah Bay, Wash., and at a gathering in that village the writer saw a woman afflicted in a manner similar to the "Ghost dance fit." A slave woman went to her, stroked her arms and head, and gradually quieted her.

The first song of this group belonged to Blue Hawk. When he gave a game this was always sung at the first "hiding."

No. 39. Blue Hawk's Hand Game Song

(Catalogue No. 1137)

Recorded by Horse Chief

Voice ♩ = 108
Drum not recorded.

Analysis.—This is an interesting example of a song with scanty melodic material and well-developed rhythm. Only two tones occur in the melody, a fundamental and its major third. The song contains, however, four phrases, the first and second having one rhythmic unit and the third and fourth another rhythmic unit. These did not vary in the renditions of the song. It will be noted that the first two phrases each contains two measures. The rests occurring in these phrases were clearly given. It is interesting to note that the first unit contains a triplet of eighth notes on the second count and the second unit contains such a triplet on the first count. The first unit contains a change of time, while the measure lengths are uniform in the second rhythmic unit.

No. 40. Hand Game Guessing Song (a)

(Catalogue No. 1138)

Recorded by Horse Chief

Voice ♩ = 108
Drum not recorded

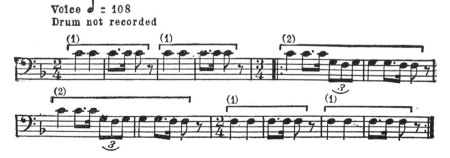

Analysis.—This song, as transcribed, is composed of three periods, each of which contains two phrases, but the latter part is repeated, making five phrases in a complete rendition. Two such complete renditions were recorded and show no differences. On the quarter notes of the first rhythmic unit there was a pulsation of the voice which can not be indicated by notation. This peculiarity was noted in other songs recorded by the same singer. It is interesting to note that a dotted eighth occurs on the accented count of the first unit and on the unaccented count of the second unit. The most prominent tones are F and C, and the song is transcribed as being in the key of F, although the third above that tone does not occur in the melody.

No. 41. Hand Game Guessing Song (b)

(Catalogue No. 1139)

Recorded by HORSE CHIEF

Voice ♩ = 60
Drum not recorded

Analysis.—Eight renditions of this song were recorded and, except in a very few instances, the sixteenth notes were given with distinctness. No words were sung and the tones were separated by the peculiar action of throat and tongue that characterizes the tone production of the Indians. The keynote appears to be F and, as the third and seventh above that tone do not appear, the song is classified as based on the first 5-toned scale. The descending fourth is a prominent interval in the framework of the melody, occurring as C to G, B flat to F, and G to D.

No. 42. Hand Game Guessing Song (c)

(Catalogue No. 1140)

Recorded by HORSE CHIEF

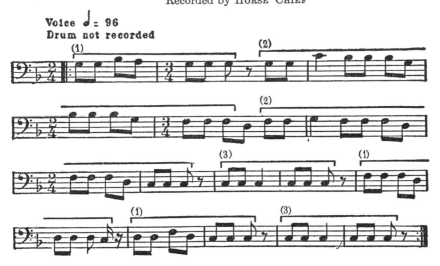

Analysis.—This song comprises three periods, each with a rhythmic unit occurring twice. There is less resemblance between these units than in many other songs. Attention is directed to the rest in the first measure of the third unit which adds interest to the melody. The only tones occurring in the song are F, G, and B flat, and the song is classified in the key of F, with the third lacking.

No. 43. Hand Game Guessing Song (d)

(Catalogue No. 1141)

Recorded by HORSE CHIEF

Analysis.—The prominence of F and C in this song suggests F as its keynote, although A occurs only once, as an unaccented tone

in the first measure.   In this, as in many other Indian songs, the classification according to a keynote is for convenience in grouping the
material and does not indicate that the song is in an established key.
The minor third D–F is prominent in the latter portion of the song.
Three rhythmic units occur but do not appear in consecutive order
as in No. 42.   The first and third units are alike except for the last
tone of the first measure, this difference being maintained in every
instance.   The principal interval is the minor third, which comprises
four-fifths of the progressions.

No. 44. Hand Game Guessing Song (e)

(Catalogue No. 1142)

Recorded by HORSE CHIEF

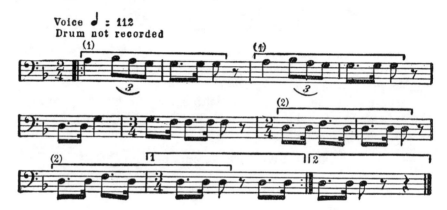

Analysis.—The framework of this melody consists of two minor
thirds, these being G–B flat and D–F.   The first of these minor
intervals comprises the first four measures of the song, with two
occurrences of the rhythmic unit.   This is followed by two measures
that may be considered connective, and the song closes with four
measures on the second named interval with a different rhythm than
that of the first phrase.   The melody tones are those of the second
5-toned scale and the downward progressions comprise two-thirds
of the entire number.   This is a proportion of descending intervals
frequently noted in Indian songs.

No. 45. Hand Game Guessing Song (f)

(Catalogue No. 1143)

Recorded by HORSE CHIEF

Voice ♩ = 96
Drum not recorded

Analysis.—The rhythm of this song is pleasing and the rhythmic unit comprises three measures. The song consists of three repetitions of this unit, the repetitions being exact in the two renditions of the song. The intonation was uncertain, as more than half the intervals are semitones which are difficult for an Indian to sing. The fourth and seventh tones of the octave are lacking as in the fourth 5-toned scale, but the song is minor in tonality.

No. 46. Hand Game Guessing Song (g)

(Catalogue No. 1144)

Recorded by HORSE CHIEF

Voice ♩ = 100
Drum not recorded

Analysis.—This song affords an example of what has been termed the influence of a rhythmic unit on that portion of the song in which it does not occur. This song comprises four periods. The first and second are repetitions of a rhythmic unit, the third differs from the unit on the last count, and the fourth, though beginning like the first period, contains one phrase like the ending of the rhythmic unit and another which resembles it but is not exactly like any other phrase in the song.   The rhythm was identical in all the renditions. The melody is less interesting than the rhythm, the first half being based on the interval of a fifth (F to C) and the last half on a fourth (D to G), with F as the principal tone of the song.

The following song was also sung while the game was in progress. In explanation it was said, "This song belonged to a man who died long ago.   He had one daughter and she died.   The old man cried every day but at last, one night, he heard a cry in the woods.   It was his daughter, who said, 'Father, I am in heaven.'   Afterwards he did not cry any more."

No. 47. "I Hear the Sound of a Child Crying"

(Catalogue No. 1098)

Recorded by EFFIE BLAIN

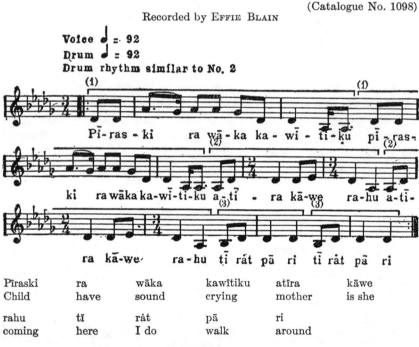

Voice ♩ = 92
Drum ♩ = 92
Drum rhythm similar to No. 2

Pīraski	ra	wāka	kawītiku	atīra	kāwe
Child	have	sound	crying	mother	is she

rahu	tī	ràt	pā	ri	
coming	here	I do	walk	around	

FREE TRANSLATION

I hear the sound of a child crying "Is my mother coming?
Here I walk around."

Analysis.—This melody is broadly outlined by the intervals of a fifth (D flat–A flat) and a fourth (A flat–D flat).   The interval of a major third does not occur and almost one-third of the intervals are fourths.   The song contains three rhythmic units occurring consecutively as in No. 42.   The first unit is the longest, the second is shorter and bears no resemblance to it, and the third is still shorter, resembling the second unit.   Drum and voice are in the same tempo.

Long ago, when the Pawnee "used to go traveling," they stopped at night to rest and frequently played the hand game.   Among them was a little boy, too young to play, who loved to watch the game. He was so little that he wore no clothing.   As soon as night came this little boy ran to get wood and made a big fire so that everyone would come and play the hand game.   He did not even want to eat he was so anxious for them to play.   The men made this song about the little boy and sang it as they played the game.

No. 48. Hand Game Song Concerning a Little Boy

(Catalogue No. 1097)

Recorded by Effie Blain

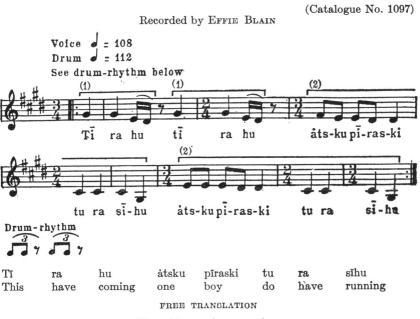

Voice ♩ = 108
Drum ♩ = 112

See drum-rhythm below

Tī   ra   hu   tī   ra   hu   àts-ku pī-ras-ki

tu   ra   sī-hu   àts-ku pī-ras-ki   tu   ra   sī-hu

Drum-rhythm

Tī	ra	hu	àtsku	pīraski	tu	ra	sīhu
This	have	coming	one	boy	do	have	running

FREE TRANSLATION

They (the men) are coming,
One boy is running.

Analysis.—Ten renditions of this song were recorded with no break in the time except a pause for breath between the eighth and ninth renditions.   It is interesting to note that the drum is slightly faster than the voice, maintaining this tempo in all the renditions. Part of the song is above and part is below the keynote.   Two rhythmic units occur, the second being much longer than the first. The song is minor in tonality and contains all the tones of the octave except the seventh.   The descent at the close of the first and second measures was given with a sliding of the voice which can not be represented in musical notation.

The next song was said to have come down from a time when only men played the hand game.

No. 49. "You Came Near Finding Them"

(Catalogue No. 1095)

Recorded by EFFIE BLAIN

Voice ♩ = 76
Drum not recorded

Analysis.—The rhythm of this song is characteristic of the physical movements of persons playing the hand game. It is a rhythm that suggests alternation and the swaying of the players from side to side. There is also an energy in the ascending approach to the first count of each measure. The tones are those of the first 5-toned scale which omits the third and seventh tones of the octave and is always a particularly free melodic form. No change of measure length occurs and the song consists entirely of repetitions of the rhythmic unit. The song contains 11 ascending and 10 descending progressions, two of each being the interval of a fourth.

A song of Roaming Chief (No. 66) was also sung at a hand game.

GHOST DANCE SONGS

The Pawnee are deeply religious by nature and received the Ghost dance with sympathy. According to Mooney "The Ghost dance was brought to the Pawnee . . . by delegates from the Arapaho and Cheyenne in the west. The doctrine made slow progress for some time, but by February, 1892, the majority of the Pawnee were dancing in confident expectation of the speedy coming of the Messiah and the buffalo. Of all these tribes the Pawnee took most interest in the new doctrine, becoming as much devoted to the Ghost dance as the Arapaho themselves." [29] A woman's Ghost dance dress is shown in Plate 8, *c*; also other costumes.

Ghost dance songs were recorded but the dance did not form a subject of study by the present writer. As stated, certain Ghost

---

[29] Mooney, James, op. cit., p. 902.

dance songs were sung in the dances at hand games while others were not used in that manner.

The hypnotic phase which the hand game has in common with the Ghost dance is indicated in the following song which was sung at the Ghost dance and also at the hand game. In old times the game and its accompanying dances were held on the prairie instead of inside a lodge. A portion of the people were called "crows," and the woman who recorded this song said that she "belonged on the crow side of the circle." At intervals these people gave the caw of the crow and imitated that bird in their dancing. (This was done in the dance connected with the hand game attended by the writer.) It is said that under the hypnotic influence of the occasion, the dancers sometimes saw a crow inside the dance circle, no one except themselves being able to see it. The singer said that she "dreamed" this song when she was a young girl.

No. 50. "The Crow"

Recorded by EFFIE BLAIN

(Catalogue No. 1087)

Voice ♩ = 116
Drum not recorded

FREE TRANSLATION

The crow, we see his likeness moving inside the circle of dancers.

Analysis.—The first two phrases of this song are based on a descending fourth and the last two phrases on a descending fifth, the repetition of these phrases comprising the entire melody. As in the preceding song, there is no change of measure length and the rhythm suggests the motion of the players. The song is minor in tonality and contains all the tones of the octave except the sixth and seventh.

The crow which sometimes appeared in the Ghost dance might speak of taking the dancer to Mother Moon or to the Ghost dance messiah. The following song was "dreamed" by the woman recording it, who said she might sing it either at a hand game or a Ghost dance.

49716°—29——7

No. 51. Song Concerning Mother Moon

(Catalogue No. 1084)

Recorded by EFFIE BLAIN

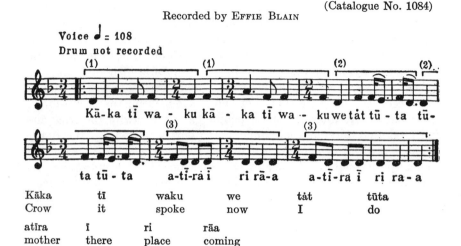

Voice ♩ = 108
Drum not recorded

Kā-ka tī wa - ku kā - ka tī wa - ku we tȧt tū - ta tū-

ta tū - ta   a-tī-rȧ ī   ri rā-a   a-tī-ra ī   ri ra - a

Kāka	tī	waku	we	tȧt	tūta
Crow	it	spoke	now	I	do

atīra	ī	ri	rāa
mother	there	place	coming

FREE TRANSLATION

The crow spoke and said, "Now I am coming to where my mother is."

Analysis.—Although this song contains three rhythmic divisions the rhythm should be studied as a whole. This song does not afford an example of thematic treatment but of carrying a rhythmic feeling from the beginning to the end of a melody. The first and second units begin with an ascending progression to an accentuated tone. It is an emphatic melody, in accordance with its words. Attention is directed to the entrance of the third rhythmic unit and the count which precedes it. The first occurrence of the second rhythmic unit shows this as an accented tone, but in this occurrence it is unaccented and leads to the strong phrases that close the song. The melodic material consists of the minor triad and second, and the song is harmonic in structure.

The next was said to be a "true song" of a boy who is now dead. He once dreamed that he was in a grave and seemed unable to free himself from this impression. Whenever this song was sung it "threw the boy into a Ghost dance fit." The words are translated, "Here is the hole, right here." The song was sung at a hand game or a Ghost dance.

Analysis.—This is a peculiar melody, not only in its use of rests but in its melodic form. Each of the two rhythmic units begins with a descent and ends with an ascending progression of a whole tone, giving rather a plaintive effect. The tone material is that of the second 5-toned scale and the song is harmonic in structure.

About one-fifth of the intervals are fourths, which is a large proportion of this interval to occur in a song that is not associated with motion. It has been noted that the fourth is especially prominent in songs connected with animals and with motion of any sort.

No. 52. Song Concerning an Open Grave

Recorded by EFFIE BLAIN

(Catalogue No. 1094)

Voice ♩ = 112
Drum ♩ = 112
Drum-rhythm similar to No. 2

The four songs next following were also said to be Ghost dance songs, used in the dances incident to a hand game.

No. 53. Ghost Dance Song (a)

Recorded by HORSE CHIEF

(Catalogue No. 1145)

Voice ♩ = 96
Drum not recorded

Analysis.—The rhythmic units of this song are simple, the second being a duplicate of the first with the addition of a closing measure.

The song comprises four periods of five measures each, the first and third being based on the descending fifth B–E, and the second and last on the descending fourth A–E. Thus it appears that E is the fundamental tone, but the third above that tone does not occur in the song. The progressions consist of 12 minor thirds and the same number of major seconds, the remaining intervals consisting of two ascending fourths and one ascending fifth.

No. 54. Ghost Dance Song (b)

(Catalogue No. 1146)

Recorded by HORSE CHIEF

Voice ♩ = 88
Drum not recorded

Analysis.—This song contains a single rhythmic unit repeated six times. The melodic progressions divide the song into three parts, each containing four measures. The compass of each part is small, the first being on the descending interval C–A flat, the second on B flat–A flat, and the third entirely on F. The rest in the first measure of the unit was clearly given. The melody progresses chiefly by whole tones, this interval constituting 8 of the 11 intervals. The melodic material consists of the minor triad and fourth.

No. 55. Ghost Dance Song (c)

(Catalogue No. 1147)

Recorded by HORSE CHIEF

Voice ♩ = 76
Drum not recorded

Analysis.—The only accented tones in this song are the keynote and fifth.   The song comprises three periods, the first and last having the same rhythmic unit and the second period having a longer unit with a change of time.   The interest and force of the song lie in the second rhythmic unit which contains a triple measure.   The first rhythmic unit begins on an unaccented tone and the second begins on an accented tone.   This peculiarity occurs also in two songs of the hand game (Nos. 43 and 47).   The song contains eight descending and only three ascending intervals.

No. 56. Ghost Dance Song (d)

(Catalogue No. 1148)

Recorded by HORSE CHIEF

Voice ♩ ≐ 96

Drum not recorded

Analysis.—In this song we feel the pathos of the Ghost dance. More than four-fifths of the intervals are semitones which occur only between F sharp and G, and D sharp and E.   Rests occur with some frequency and were given uniformly in all the renditions.   It is interesting to compare the close of the first rhythmic unit with that of the second which contains the same count division with a different accent.

This and the succeeding song were not used in the hand game. The singer said that he composed this song when waking from a trance in the Ghost dance.   He dreamed of a yellow star which came to him and said, "I am the star which you see in the sky at night." The star was in the form of a woman holding in her hand an eagle feather painted yellow.   She gave him the feather, saying, "All the stars in the sky are people."   A dream of the yellow star was induced by watching the star when in a Ghost dance trance.   The favor of "yellow star" was greatly desired as she does not appear to many dancers, but she gives to her favored friends the right to wear a yellow eagle feather upright in their hair and to use it in hypnotizing other dancers.   If such a feather is used under a false pretense no results can be obtained.

No. 57. "The Yellow Star"

Recorded by WICITA BLAIN

(Catalogue No. 1107)

Voice ♩ = 84
Drum ♩ = 84
Drum rhythm similar to No. 26

Fine

FREE TRANSLATION

The yellow star has noticed me,
Furthermore it gave me a standing yellow feather,
That yellow star.

Analysis.—Although the compass of this melody is only five tones it contains three rhythmic units. On comparing these we note that the second unit extends the use of the dotted eighth, which occurs in the first unit, and that the third unit contains the dotted eighth and also the triplet which occurs in the first unit. This thematic development is interesting and somewhat unusual. The rhythm did not vary in the four renditions. The connecting phrase did not occur between the second and third renditions. Progression is chiefly by whole tones and the song is harmonic in structure.

The man to whom the next song belonged was Running Scout, a man who was very religious and remained in a Ghost dance trance for several days. His friends thought him unbalanced but when he awoke he told them that he had been to the Messiah who told him to "go to the village." Following this instruction, he saw many men dancing. Some had fox skins around their heads while others used fox skins in hypnotizing their fellow dancers. For this reason Running Scout always wore a fox skin in the Ghost dance. The skin was not made into a cap but the head and tail were fastened together and hung at the back of his neck in such a manner that the tail rested on his shoulder. He also gave the call of the fox while he was dancing.

No. 58. Running Scout's Ghost Dance Song

(Catalogue No. 1088)

Recorded by EFFIE BLAIN

Voice ♩ = 96
Drum not recorded

Īrehe	wēi	sārit	kēwaku	rī	rāraha
Now there	they	are	fox	they	have

Analysis.—This song, like others of the hand game and Ghost dance, consists of repetitions of the rhythmic unit. In this instance there are two units, the second occurring only in the middle part of the song. It is interesting to compare the third measure from the beginning with the second measure from the close, the ascent to the accented tone in the first instance expressing a certain restlessness while the second phrase is more restful. This song contains the minor triad and fourth and progresses chiefly by whole tones.

The final song of this group is concerning the Ghost dance and, according to Mr. Murie, was sung in the Young Dog Society. The words "the father's child" refer to the messiah whose coming was expected in the Ghost dance.

Analysis.—The three renditions of this song are alike in every respect except that the intonation on D in the upper octave is variable, occasionally being sung almost as D sharp. The time was maintained steadily and the renditions were separated by shrill cries. The song comprises two periods, the first containing eight and the second containing seven measures. Two rhythmic units occur, the second being an extension of the first. The song has a compass of 12 tones, which is somewhat unusual in Pawnee songs.

No. 59. Song Concerning the Ghost Dance

(Catalogue No. 1102)

Recorded by WICITA BLAIN

Wī	ra	ha	ī	ra	ha	ti	wēri
There	coming	yonder	it	coming	yonder	this	now
hāk	tsa	atīas	pīraū	kūra	hāk [30]	kux	
stick	lies	father	child	his	stick	his	
tī	ku	hāk	kux	ī	ra	ha	
he	to me	stick	his	it	coming	yonder	

FREE TRANSLATION

There it is lying yonder, this stick lying here,
The father's own child gave it to me,
It is coming yonder.

MAN CHIEF'S SONGS

The singer spoke with deep affection of Man Chief, to whom many songs were attributed. According to the singer, Man Chief was chief of the four bands of Pawnee and died in 1858 at the age of 74 years. Concerning the next song it was said, "When we first elected Man Chief as chief he thanked God, and then he sang this song."

---

[30] The last letter of this word was omitted by the singer.

The words with the repetition of the melody were: "My father himself, through him I am exalted (made prominent) among the people."

No. 60. "I am Exalted Among the People"

(Catalogue No. 1123)

Recorded by JOHN LUWAK

Voice ♩ = 60
Drum not recorded

Atīås	ru	a	ra	rike
Father	yonder	is said	to have	stood

Analysis.—This song is unique in containing only two ascending progressions. It has a compass of 10 tones and contains all the tones of the octave except the sixth. Attention is directed to the fourth measure, which is the only one not containing the rhythmic unit. This measure, by its slight difference from the rhythmic unit, swings the rhythm of the entire song and avoids the monotony that would follow if the rhythmic unit were continuously repeated. Progression is chiefly by whole tones.

Man Chief received numerous songs in dreams. The first song is a war dance of the Iruska, it being said that the "spirits told him about this dance, which is different from an ordinary war dance." This society corresponds to the Hethushka of the Omaha, a society of distinguished warriors. Before recording this song Luwak recorded the following sentences: "The song which I am about to sing belonged to Man Chief. When he became a chief he used to go out into the storm and stand first in one place and then in another. He heard Tirawa speak through the clouds. He knew the heavens were the ruling power and prayed for his people." While speaking, he beat the drum in the same tempo as in the song which followed.

Analysis.—The man who recorded this song had recently taken part in a ceremony which lasted several days and was hoarse from singing on that occasion. To this may be attributed a lack of accuracy in the repetitions of his song. Transcription is from the last renditions, in which the intonation was clearest. The song has a compass of 10 tones, beginning on the highest and ending on the lowest tone of the compass. After descending to the lowest tone with repetitions of the rhythmic unit the melody ascends to the fifth and again descends to the lowest tone, this time in a different rhythm. The whole tone comprises two-thirds of the progressions.

No. 61. "The Heavens Are Speaking"

(Catalogue No. 1122)

Recorded by JOHN LUWAK

Rū	tåt	lū	ra	wē	riku	wē	rix
Did	I	did	have	around	stands	now	they
wāwak	tiku	he	ris	ta	kitāwiu		
speaking	they are	now	you	have	ruling power		

(In repetitions of the song)

Nihuksu	tåt		titska	wītasi	kitāwiu
Only	I		one mind	then	ruling power
he	rix	ti	rus	ta	kawāhát
now	they	this	you	have	heavens

FREE TRANSLATION

I stood here, I stood there,
The clouds are speaking,
I say, "You are the ruling power,
I do not understand, I only know what I am told,
You are the ruling power, you are now speaking,
This power is yours, O heavens."

The next song contains the same idea of the "ruling power in the heavens."

No. 62. "O Expanse of the Heavens"

(Catalogue No. 1129)

Recorded by JOHN LUWAK

Voice ♩ = 104
Drum not recorded

Īri	hawa	wī	tas	ta	kitawi	ras
There	almost always	are	you	have	powers (or leaders)	you

ta	kāwaha	ki	wē	tas	ta	kītawi
have	heavens	expand	are	you	have	powers

FREE TRANSLATION

I believe that in you, O heavens, dwell the ruling powers.

Analysis.—This song is major in tonality and contains one accidental, the fourth raised a semitone. The rhythm presents an unusual monotony as the only count-divisions, except in the final measures, are dotted quarter notes followed by eighth notes. The song has a compass of an octave and progresses by a variety of intervals.

The song next following was used as an old war dance.

It was the custom of the young men, in former times, to make known that they had arrived at an age of realization and had "put their trust in the heavens." James R. Murie said that he, as a young man, went around the village singing this song with other young men, so that all the people might hear and know they had assumed the attitude of men toward life. It is an Iruska but not a dancing song and belonged to Man Chief.

Analysis.—With a range of 10 tones this song contains the tone material of the second 5-toned scale. As in several other songs with large compass, it begins on the highest tone of its compass and ends on the lowest. The song consists of four periods, the third differing slightly from the others in rhythm, a form which occurs frequently in the simpler songs of the Indians.

No. 63. "Power is in the Heavens"

(Catalogue No. 1130)

Recorded by JOHN LUWAK

Voice ♩ = 104
Drum ♩ = 126
Drum-rhythm similar to No. 26

FREE TRANSLATION

My spirit rests in the belief that power is in the heavens.

No. 64. "Our Hearts Are Set in the Heavens"

(Catalogue No. 1080)

Recorded by EFFIE BLAIN

Voice ♩ = 84
Drum not recorded

Ru tē ra___ ri - hū-ku   ru tē ra___ ri - hū-ku tsik-

su hē_ ra_ tū-ta a tī re__ wa - hā-ke

Ru	tē	ra	rihuku	tsiksu	hē	ra
There	is	have	only	spirit	or	have

tūta	a	tī	re	wahāke		
upon	and	this	have	expanse of the heavens		

FREE TRANSLATION

It is there that our hearts are set,
In the expanse of the heavens.

Analysis.—In rhythmic form this song is like the song next preceding, the third period containing a change of rhythm. The song contains 12 descending and 6 ascending progressions, a proportion which occurs so frequently in Indian songs that it may be said to be characteristic. In all renditions the second tone is sharped, which introduces the interval of a semitone, and was sung with distinctness. The song contains no change of measure lengths and has a compass of 13 tones, beginning on the highest and ending on the lowest tone of this compass.

The final song belonging to Man Chief is similar to those already presented, though the words are not translated.

No. 65. Man Chief's Song

(Catalogue No. 1131)

Recorded by JOHN LUWAK

Voice ♩ = 63.
Drum ♩ = 63
Drum-rhythm similar to No. 2

Analysis.—The rhythmic form of this song is interesting and complete. The song contains two rhythmic units, the second being the opening phrase of the first unit and occurring at the close of the song. In structure the song is harmonic. It is minor in tonality, has a compass of an octave, and progresses by a variety of intervals, those occurring most frequently being the fourth and the major second.

ROAMING CHIEF'S SONGS

The two songs next following belonged to a comparatively recent chief of the Chaui Band. The grief of his wife at the death of a daughter is mentioned in connection with her song (No. 83). Roaming Chief was hereditary chief of this band and was a nephew of the famous Pitalesaru, who was appointed chief of the confederated bands of the Pawnee by the Government of the United States.

It was said that "Tirawa had pity on Roaming Chief" and that, during a Ghost dance, he fell in a trance. Visions appeared to him in this trance, the present song referring to such an experience. A Ghost dance was sometimes held especially for Roaming Chief and he "cried as he sang this song." It was also customary to sing this song at a hand game.

Analysis.—This song is in a form already noted, the third period being in rhythm different from that of the first, second, and fourth. The compass is 13 tones and more than half the progressions are

whole tones and semitones. The seventh is sharped in every occurrence, this accidental being of particular interest in a song with
minor tonality. The song contains all the tones of the octave except
the fourth and sixth.

No. 66. "It Is Good Where We Are Now"

(Catalogue No. 1090)

Recorded by EFFIE BLAIN

Ra	hi	he	hĕru	kītu	tix	wakīa
Yonder	there	they	come	are	they	saying
ahu	tīhe	we	tūrahe	hi	he	hĕru
	over here	now	good	there	they	come

FREE TRANSLATION

There they come yonder,
They are saying "It is good over here
where we are now."
There they come.

Roaming Chief sang the following song at the Pipe dance and it
was sung at the Victory dance attended by the writer. It was
said that "Mother Corn was carried on the warpath to give victory
and was also used in the Pipe dance." The words are freely translated, "My whole trust is in Mother Corn."

Analysis.—The tempo of this song was slow and somewhat *rubato*,
a slight prolonging of certain tones being indicated in the transcription. In some of the renditions the time values in the third

measure were changed to conform to different words but the duration
of the measure remained the same.   The song contains 19 intervals,
10 of which are whole tones and 5 are fourths.

No. 67. "My Trust is in Mother Corn"

(Catalogue No. 1089)

Recorded by JOHN LUWAK

Voice ♩ = 53
Drum not recorded

SONGS OF AFFECTION

Songs rising from deep affection and respect were occasionally
sung by Indians in the old times, and might be concerning persons
who had been married for many years.   The distinction between these
and the modern "love song" is clearly drawn by the Indians and is
evident from the words of the songs.   The Sioux said that in old
times they had a few songs concerning a man's qualification to wed,
this being determined by his success in war or on the buffalo hunt.[31]
Otter Woman, an aged widow of the Mandan Tribe, recorded songs
of loneliness for her husband, and two very old songs expressing a
gentle longing.   These were sung by young girls when at work in the
gardens and are as delicate as the little plants which they tended so
carefully.[32]   The cause of the change from these songs of respectful
affection to the modern "love song" is found in the general change
from primitive customs.

In former times the marriages of young people were either arranged
by the parents or subject to parental approval.   A period of transition began when the young people refused to recognize parental authority in the matter of their affections.   This led to clandestine meetings.
A few songs of this period were recorded among the Sioux, one containing the words "If you are truthful, come. Walks Visibly (woman's
name) has said this."[33]   The words of modern Indian love songs
usually express a lack of respect for women, and often boast of fas-
cinations and conquests.   They are connected with intoxication and are
sung by young men of no standing among their own people.   Many

---

[31] Teton Sioux Music, p. 370.
[32] Mandan and Hidatsa Music, pp. 54-57.
[33] Teton Sioux Music, p. 510.

such songs have been recorded among the Chippewa and Menominee. The development of this class of songs among the Pawnee is considered in a subsequent paragraph.

Three of the old songs of affection were obtained among the Pawnee, the first two being recorded by John Luwak, chief of the Chaui Band, while his wife assisted with the information. As already stated, the marriages were formerly arranged by the parents and "the fathers usually took charge of the matter." It was further said that "the marriages always turned out happily as the old people knew better than the young people and understood which boys and girls would get along the best." Mrs. Luwak, wife of the singer, said that her marriage was arranged by her parents and that at first she "cried every day," but she indicated with some shyness that the marriage had resulted happily.

The following is the song of a man who is going to war. He addresses his wife, saying, "When I die do not cry unless you really loved me, but if you love me you will cry and you will not remarry soon after I die."

No. 68. Song of Affection (a)

(Catalogue No. 1136)

Recorded by JOHN LUWAK

Analysis.—The third tone in this song was followed by a downward *glissando* of about a tone which is impossible to transcribe. It is interesting to note that the count divisions of the first unit are reversed in the second unit, a thematic treatment showing the intelligence of the Indian musician. The song is major in tonality, has a compass of 10 tones, and about 80 per cent of the progressions are major seconds. Three renditions were recorded without a break in the time.

In explanation of the next song it was said, "There was once a married couple. One day the wife said to her husband, 'I love you very much and if you should die I would cry every day.' This was the first time that either had admitted an affection for the other."

No. 69. Song of Affection (b)

(Catalogue No. 1135)

Recorded by JOHN LUWAK

Voice ♩ = 138
Drum not recorded

Analysis.—The present song is unusual in that the intonation on single phrases was good while the transition from one phrase to another was uncertain in intonation. This may have been due to the compass of two octaves, the rapid tempo, and the agitation in the mind of the singer. The rhythmic unit is simple and its repetitions comprise practically the entire song. In every rendition there was a pause after the sixth measure, followed by a repetition of these six measures, and a continuance without a break in the time. All the tones of the octave except the seventh are present in this remarkable melody.

There is deep pathos in the next song and its history. A woman composed this song while her husband was on the warpath. She died during his absence, but her friends had learned the song. When her husband returned they sang the song and told him its story. He learned the song.

49716°—29——8

No. 70. Song of a Warrior's Wife

(Catalogue No. 1100)

Recorded by Effie Blain

Voice ♪= 144 (♩= 72)
Drum not recorded

FREE TRANSLATION

I wonder where he is sitting,
That person who comes and sits in my tipi.

Analysis.—In all renditions of this song the 7–8 and 3–4 measures were sung in exact time. Except for one minor third the melody progresses entirely by fourths and major seconds. It has a compass of 10 tones and contains the entire octave except the fourth.

Mr. James R. Murie and other old members of the tribe said that love songs, in the white man's use of that term, were unknown among the better class of Pawnee in the early days. According to Mr. Murie, there were four classes of Pawnee, the lowest being considered outcasts by the remainder of the tribe. These people camped near towns and worked for white people, from whom they obtained whisky. This class of Pawnee sang what were termed "crazy people's songs," which were associated with "love charms" and evil influences. No effort was made to secure examples of these songs. A change from the former attitude toward women, however, is shown in the following song which was said to be very old. It is not of so low a character as the "crazy people's songs," neither does it represent the high standard of life indicated in the former songs of this group. A girl married a man for whom she did not care and it would appear that, instead of adapting himself to the situation, he sought consolation elsewhere.

Analysis.—This melody consists of two parts, the first of which contains the rhythmic unit. The second part begins with a succession of eighth notes, followed by a measure which preserves the count divisions of the rhythmic unit. The count divisions throughout the song were sung with special clearness. The song is transcribed as having B flat for its keynote but the third above that tone does not occur. Except for an ascending octave the only in-

tervals are fourths and major seconds.   Drum and voice are different
in tempo, each being maintained with regularity.

No. 71. "Other Girls Are as Pretty as She"

(Catalogue No. 1101)

Recorded by EFFIE BLAIN

Voice ♩ = 112
Drum ♩ = 120
Drum-rhythm similar to No. 2

A modern love song (not transcribed) was translated as follows:
"That lady loves me.   I bet she is thinking of me."   It was said to
be the song of a man already married who wanted the person mentioned in the song to elope with him.

Songs of this class were preceded by the syllable *ee–ee* on a low tone
in imitation of a flute.   The informant said "the flute was courting
medicine of a bad kind."

MYTHS AND FOLK TALES

The Pawnee possessed many stories pertaining to the origin of
sacred bundles and the doings of mythological persons.   Concerning
such stories Doctor Dorsey states: "These tales, as a rule, are told
only during ceremonies, especially during the intermissions or pauses
in the ceremony which occur from time to time between rites, or
during resting periods in the chanting of a long ritual.   During such
intermissions anyone of those present may ask the priests for
such a tale.   Especially is it the privilege of the one who has made
the ceremony possible, by providing the food for the sacrifice and
feast, to ask that such a tale be related.   These tales may also, under
certain circumstances, be told outside the ceremonial lodge . . . and
the chief object in relating them is to furnish instruction." [34]   Such
stories gradually passed into current knowledge and were told as
folk tales by any member of the tribe without mention of their
religious significance.

---

[34] Dorsey, The Pawnee: Mythology (Pt. 1), Carnegie Institution of Washington, Publ. No. 59, Washington, 1906.

The first three stories of the following group are versions of old legends connected with the mythology of the tribe, while the fourth story in the group appears to be an ordinary folk tale. It differs from the others in that the entire narrative was sung. (Cf. Rudimentary Songs, Northern Ute music, pp. 200–205.)

In the first story we find an interesting resemblance to a story recorded in southern Arizona.[35]

STORY OF THE GAMBLER
RELATED BY FANNIE CHAPMAN

In a certain village were two young boys. They were good-looking lads and wore their hair long on the right side of the head. One day the younger boy thought he would go to another village in the woods. When he came near this village he saw the smoke of a tipi that stood by itself among the willows. He went there and stood outside the entrance.

In this tipi lived an old woman and her three granddaughters. The old woman told the youngest girl to go outside and see if anyone was there. The girl saw the strange lad and returned, saying, "O grandmother, there is a good-looking young man outside." The old woman went to speak with him and said, "You had better go to some village where the people have more money. We are very poor." But the lad replied, "No. I came here and this is where I belong." The old woman said, "Well, come in," and the boy entered the tipi. Later the old woman said, "You had better go away for the chief of our band is very unkind to strangers. You must watch, for Longnose (Coyote) will come before daylight to see if anyone is here. He will see you and tell the chief, who will ask you to breakfast. If he offers you dry pumpkin do not eat it, nor corn, nor mush. Bring it home with you."

Before daylight, as the old woman had predicted, Coyote came to see if anyone was in the tipi. The old woman said, "See my grandson, how good-looking he is. He ought to go where the big men are." Coyote ran at once to the chief and said, "O chief, there is a good looking young man down at the old woman's tipi. When you kill him he will be the leader of your heads." (Referring to a row of the heads of men killed by the chief that had been put in his tipi.) The chief said, "Run down to the old woman's tipi and bring the young man. I want to feast him." Coyote ran as fast as he could. The old woman saw him coming and again told the young man not to eat anything but to bring the food home. Coyote said to the young man, "You certainly are good-looking." When the chief saw the young man he said, "I sent for you to eat with me," and offered him dry

---

[35] Story of the Gambler, Papago Music, Bull. 90, Bur. Amer. Ethn., pp. 35–54. Cf. also Dorsey, op. cit., pp. 185–191.

pumpkin, corn, mush, and other food. The lad replied, "O grandfather, I am full; I have had my breakfast; I will take this home to
my grandmother." Coyote went with him and waited while the old
woman emptied and washed the bowls. Then Coyote took the bowls
back to the chief. After the boy refused to eat the food, the chief
wanted him to play the "stick game."[36] He refused at first but
finally he said that he would play in two days, saying he must wait
because he was so tired. The chief said, "Choose a day and we will
play." The boy went home and told the old woman that he was
to play the stick game with the chief. She said, "O my boy, you
did wrong to consent. You saw those heads in the chief's tent.
He will kill you and all our people."

Before daylight on the day of the game Coyote opened the old
woman's door and said, "The chief is at the place for the game, he is
waiting for you." The boy replied, "I will go when I am ready."
Later they began to play the stick game. The boy had people on his
side and also a bird-man (bird turned into a man), who watched
everything. Coyote watched everything on the chief's side. The
boy had nothing to wager so he bet the people who were on his side,
and at last he was obliged to bet himself. The old chief won, so the
people on the chief's side killed all the people on the boy's side. They
even killed the boy. Then they cut off all the heads and put them
up with the other heads in the chief's lodge.

While this was happening the elder of the two boys, mentioned at
the beginning of this story, grew uneasy about his brother. He
determined to find him and traced him to the village, then he went
home, got his bow and arrows, and went to the old woman's tipi.
The old woman did as before, sending the same girl to see if anyone
were outside. The girl returned and said, "It looks as though that
good-looking boy had come to life." The old woman invited him
into the tent but said as before, "O my grandson, why do you come

---

[36] In the story of "Blood-clot boy," Doctor Dorsey described the boy as making a ring of ash stick which
he wound with a string made of boiled buffalo hide so that it looked like a spider's web. The grandmother
rolled the ring and the boy shot it with arrows and killed buffalo. The same authority states that "The
ring and javelin game . . . was originally played for the direct purpose of calling the buffalo. . . . The two
sticks represent young buffalo bulls which turned into the gaming sticks, leaving first full instructions as
to how they were to be treated, how the game was to be played, how the songs were to be sung, and how
they were to be anointed with the buffalo fat. The ring, according to the story, was originally a buffalo
cow." (Traditions of the Skidi Pawnee, pp. 84, 344.)

Maj. Stephen H. Long witnessed the playing of this game and described it as follows: "The instruments
used are a small hoop about 6 inches in diameter, which is usually wound with thongs of leather, and a pole
5 or 6 feet long, on the larger end of which a limb is left to project about 6 inches. . . . The game is played
upon a smooth beaten path, at one end of which the gamester commences, and running at full speed, he
first rolls from him the hoop, then discharges after it the pole, which slides along the path pursuing the
hoop until both stop together, at the distance of about 30 yards from the place whence they were thrown.
After throwing them from him the gamester continues his pace and the Indian, the hoop, and the pole
arrive at the end of the path about the same time. The effort appears to be to place the end of the pole
either in the ring, or as near as possible, and we could perceive that those casts were considered best when
the ring was caught by the hook at the end of the pole." (James, Edwin, Account of an Expedition from
Pittsburg to the Rocky Mountains under command of Maj. Stephen H. Long, Vol. I, p. 444. Philadelphia,
1823.)

here. You ought to go where the rich people are." He replied as
his brother had done, "No, I want to be here." They were so poor
that they gave him only one bean from those they had gathered.
At night the old woman said as before, "O my grandson, I wish you
would go away. Go somewhere else or go home, for someone will
come early in the morning to look all around the place."

Everything happened exactly as before. Coyote came, found the
young man, and took him to the chief, who offered him food. The
young man replied, as his brother had done, that he was not hungry,
and he took the food home. The chief asked him to play the stick
game and he said that he was too tired to play that day. It was
decided that they would play in a few days. The boy went home and
said to his grandmother, "I am going to play the stick game with the
chief. To-morrow I want you to clean up the house and put everything one side, then I want you all to go into the woods. Do not try to
look into the house until I call you." Then he asked, "Is there
any place around here where the people used to kill buffalo?" She
replied, "Yes, over there by the hill."

After they had gone the young man took the pipe out of the sacred
bundle that the old woman kept. Before daylight he filled the pipe
and went toward the place where they used to kill the buffalo. When
he reached the place he found many buffalo bones. He held the
stem of the pipe down toward the buffalo bones and sang the following
song.

No. 72. Folk Tale Song (a)

(Catalogue No. 1157)

Recorded by FANNIE CHAPMAN

Voice ♩ = 116
Drum not recorded

FREE TRANSLATION

"Father, I have brought this pipe for you to smoke. I am lonely for my
brother."

Analysis.—The interval of a fourth constitutes 68 per cent of the intervals in this song, which is an unusually large proportion of this interval.   The song is harmonic in structure and contains the complete octave except the second and seventh.   The rhythmic structure is interesting as the three rhythmic units occur in somewhat irregular order.

As the young man sang this song the bones came to life and made a noise like a great many buffalo.   He said, "Now, fathers, grandfathers and grandmothers, I want you to pity me.   That is why I sang."   They replied, "All right."   Then a middle-aged buffalo with shining horns came toward him and said, "I will be the first to help you.   We know about that wicked chief and what he has been doing."   The buffalo threw himself down and when he got up he shook himself.   Where he had been lying the boy saw a game stick.   The buffalo said, "Take that stick."   A young buffalo did the same and gave the boy another stick.   Then a young buffalo cow did the same and when she arose the boy saw a game ring which she told him to use.   The boy brought the two sticks and the ring home with him and hung them beside the sacred bundle.   On the day of the game he told his grandmother that he would send someone for the sticks and the ring but did not want anyone to be at home when the messenger came.

In the morning Coyote came as before and said that all was ready for the game.   Everything was the same as when the younger man played, the chief having Coyote and the man having the bird-man on his side.   They began to play and the chief won as before.   The boy had no goods so he bet the people, as his brother had done.   The chief said, "Now you have bet all the people, you ought to bet yourself."   The young man said "All right."   Then his stick struck the chief's stick and broke it in two.   The young man said, "Thanks. Now I will not be killed."   The chief said, "Perhaps you have some gaming sticks somewhere."   The man said, "Yes," and sent Coyote to get them, adding, "They are common sticks, lying on the floor."   Coyote went to the old woman's lodge, opened the door and heard a noise as of many buffalo.   He was frightened and ran back.   The chief sent another messenger, who brought the same report.   Then the boy sent the bird-man, who brought the sticks and the ring.   They did not make any noise when he entered the lodge for they knew he was the right person.

The boy played with the sticks and had good luck.   He won back all the people, and the chief's leg was broken.   Then the boy sang this song.

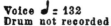

No. 73. Folk Tale Song (b)

(Catalogue No. 1158)

Recorded by FANNIE CHAPMAN

Voice ♩ = 132
Drum not recorded

FREE TRANSLATION

"You are a good gambler. They say you are a good gambler. Get up and play."

Analysis.—This song comprises four periods, the rhythm being the same in each. The descent of the voice at the close of each phrase was somewhat *glissando* but kept the intervals with reasonable distinctness. The song is melodic in structure and contains all the tones of the octave except the fourth.

They played again and the chief said, "Throw the sticks toward the east." They threw the sticks toward the east and the boy's stick went through the hoop and went on and on, and finally it turned into a buffalo. As soon as the chief's people saw the stick turn into a buffalo they began to cry, but the boy's people began to rejoice.

The young man asked, "Where is my brother's head?" They told him. He asked, "Where are his bones?" They told him this also. Then he laid his brother's bones in order on the ground, with the head at one end. Then he stood below his brother's foot and kicked the foot, saying, "Why are you sleeping so long?" His brother arose and said, "Yes, I have been asleep a long time," and smoothed his hair.

They killed the chief where the game had been played and they killed all the chief's people.

Then the two brothers returned to their own village.

STORY OF COYOTE AND THE TURKEYS [37]

RELATED BY MRS. MARY MURIE

There was a village and a man who used to run around by himself. He was Coyote. He went and sat on a hill looking down and he saw a big flock of turkeys. He was hungry, as coyotes always are, and he thought, "I am going to get one of them." So he went down. The turkeys nudged each other and said, "There comes a

---

[37] Cf. "Coyote and the turkeys," Dorsey, Traditions of the Skidi Pawnee, p. 265. Also story of Wenabojo and the ducks, Chippewa Music, p. 206. Although there is a similarity in these stories of the Pawnee and Chippewa there is no resemblance in the song which was sung in connection with the story.

thief. He looks hungry. We must look out for him. He is tricky."
They all said that. Coyote said to the turkeys, "Grandchildren,
let us have a little game." The turkeys said, "What kind of a game
are we going to have?" Coyote said, "Well, don't let us have a
game, let us have a dance." The turkeys said, "All right, let us
have a dance."

Coyote looked at the turkeys. Some were big, fat ones. He
selected about six of the biggest and fattest and said, "You must
stand in front." Then he arranged two rows back of them. Then he
said, "I have a song. While you dance you must close your eyes.
When I begin to sing you must all close your eyes." He kept his
eyes open and he saw one turkey with its eyes open. He said, "Close
your eyes, you are looking at me." He sang again, and after a while
he saw they all had their eyes shut. He had a club in his hand but
he kept on singing. The turkeys all had their eyes shut and he
killed all in the front row. The rest flew away before he could kill
them. Then he said that he would have a feast for his wives and
his children. He said, "Turkeys have not much sense."

No. 74. Song of Coyote

Recorded by MARY MURIE

(Catalogue No. 1154)

Voice $\boldsymbol{\downarrow}$ = 100
Drum not recorded

FREE TRANSLATION

Put your heads down, move your hips as you dance

Analysis.—The rhythm of this song is continuous from the first
measure to the last, and is especially interesting in the latter portion.
Attention is directed to the effective use of a triple measure followed
by a double measure at the close of the melody. The tones occurring
in the song are G and A, D and E, occurring in whole-toned progressions. The last two notes were sung to the syllables "tut, tut,"
supposed to represent the cry of the turkeys.

The narrator of the next story said that it did not originate with the
Pawnee and she thought that it came from the Omaha in Nebraska.

STORY OF NURI AND HIS BROTHER

RELATED BY MRS. MARY MURIE

There was a man so jealous of his wife that he determined to take
her away from the village. He told her to pack everything and
they would go. They took plenty of dried meat, pounded meat,
corn, and all kinds of food, and left the village. When night came

they camped. They were far from any people and her husband said they would stay in that place. He was a good hunter and killed deer, turkeys, and other game. After a while they made an earth lodge to live in. Every morning the man put plenty of meat beside the fire, brought some water, and told his wife to stay in the lodge until his return. He was gone until night.

In time his wife bore a child and named it Nuri. Indeed she bore twin boys, but her husband did not notice the second child and buried it with the afterbirth. The second child crawled out of the ground and lived with the animals, but his mother never knew. Her husband told her, as before, that she must stay in the lodge. He said that he had seen some bad people prowling about. One day, when the man was away, these bad people came to the lodge. His wife was sitting beside the fire and the baby was asleep when she heard a sound and looked toward the door. Seven men entered the lodge and said, "Give us something to eat. We know that you have plenty of food." She did not reply but pointed to the meat that was cooking on sticks around the fire. They ate it all and went away. After they had gone she exclaimed, "Those horrid men ate all my meat." One heard it and said to the others, "She called us names." So they all went into the lodge and killed her. They did not see the baby but they carried the woman's body to their camp and devoured it. When the man came home he looked for his wife, and seeing the tracks he knew the wicked people had taken her. The man grieved greatly for his wife.

By this time the baby was old enough to walk and talk. Every morning before the man went to hunt he fixed the meat ready to cook and told the little boy to play inside the lodge. One day he went away as usual, after fixing the meat, and the little boy thought, "I will go outside. I never have seen what it is like out there." He went out and saw a little boy coming toward him. The boy was about his own size and was singing the following song.

No. 75. Song of the Strange Little Boy

(Catalogue No. 1155)

Recorded by Mary Murie

Voice ♩ = 76
Drum not recorded
Irregular in tonality

Analysis.—This song is classified as irregular in tonality. The only progressions are whole tones and fourths, and the sequence of tones can scarcely be said to suggest a keynote. Both the melody and rhythm are simple and childish.

The strange boy (who was his brother) said, "Nuri, you are having a good time with your father but I am here with my grandmothers, the wood rats. Your father is my father too. I have plenty of wild grapes and cherries but I do not have any meat to eat." Nuri said, "Come into the lodge and I will give you some." The strange boy sniffed the air and asked, "Is your father here?" "No," said Nuri. The strange boy went into the lodge and played until it was time for their father to return. Then he ran away, saying, "Forget, forget," so that Nuri would not tell their father. This child was a "wonder boy" and he came every day until both boys were quite grown. One day he failed to say "Forget" when he went away. As the boy and his father were eating their supper Nuri said, "Father, I want to tell you something. There is a little boy who comes every day to play with me while you are away." The man said to himself, "I will try to catch the boy." So one morning he hid instead of going away. The wonder boy came as usual, singing the same little song. He stopped and sniffed the air, saying to Nuri, "Your father is here." "No," said Nuri, "Perhaps you smell his blanket." "It is certainly he," said the boy, and ran away. The father determined to catch the boy by a trick and told Nuri how to tie a thong around his brother's scalplock. In the struggle that ensued the wonder-boy's scalplock was torn from his head and held by the thong. The father kept the scalplock gave the boys a good supper, and told them to stay in the lodge.

Nuri obeyed his father, but as time passed, his brother continually tried to lead him into danger. When Nuri objected his brother would say, "Give me my hair and I will go back to my grandmothers." Then Nuri would yield, but the boys always returned in safety. One day they brought snake rattles and hung them on the door of the lodge. Another day they went to a place where a boat was moored. If anyone went in this boat it upset, threw the people into the water, and then returned to its place by the shore. The wonder boy wanted to go in the boat but Nuri objected. The boy said as before, "Then you must give me my hair and I will go back to my grandmothers." Nuri yielded and they went in the boat, which soon began tipping endwise and sidewise. "Do as I do," cried the wonder-boy, moving his arms and making a noise like a wild goose. Nuri imitated him and the boys flew away. Before leaving the boat they sang the following song.

No. 76. Song as the Boys Flew Away

(Catalogue No. 1156)

Recorded by MARY MURIE

Voice ♩ = 69
Drum not recorded

FREE TRANSLATION

Nuri, do this and we will turn into geese.   We will not drown.

Analysis.—No ascending progressions occur in this melody, which contains the tones of the fourth 5-toned scale. It is harmonic in structure and has a rhythmic unit. Although the melody is short it has an interesting and characteristic rhythm.

After they flew away the boat returned to the landing.

Then the wonder boy wanted to go where the people lived who killed his mother. These people lived in straw huts and when they saw the boys they said, "These boys are fat; we will have a good feast." The wonder boy heard them talking. They called to the boys and said, "Come in soon, we will have the feast ready," and aside they said, "The boys have no sense." Nuri was afraid but his brother said, "Do not cry. We will destroy them. If we do not they will kill us." The boys went into the lodge and saw a kettle full of boiling water. The wonder boy said, "Do as I do." Then both boys jumped on the edge of the kettle and upset it. The boiling water fell on the people but the boys flew out of the lodge like burned leaves. The people fought and killed one another, thinking they were killing the boys, and the lodge burned up. These people had long sharp bones at the points of their elbows and heels and on the back of their heads. When they were dead the boys took off three or four of these points. The wonder boy said, "Let us take these home for father to use in sewing moccasins."

This frightened the father and that night he made up his mind to run away and leave the boys. The wonder boy knew that his father would do this but Nuri cried the next morning, when his father had gone. The brother said, "Father has left us but we will search until we find him." So the boys started to find their father. At first they saw no trace, and whenever they met a snake, a bear, or even a little bug the wonder boy would ask, "Have you seen my father?"

They replied "No." After the boys had traveled a long time the brother said to Nuri, "Are you tired?" Nuri said that he was tired, and his brother summoned a tiger (mountain lion?) and both boys rode on his back. When they had traveled a long way farther they came to a village and asked, "Have you seen our father?" The people replied, "Yes, we saw him going north." The boys traveled all that night but could not find him. The brother said, "Let us kill all the people in every village." Nuri cried, but yielded. The wonder boy said, "Nuri, do this." The boys turned their heads from side to side and they rattled. They said to the people, "If you see us you will die, and if you do not see us you will die." The people fell over and died, one after another. Then the boys looked all through the village but could not find their father. At the third village they found that their father had been killed by the people. Nuri cried but his brother said, "I would not cry. He left us to starve." They found their father's body and took it away to a high hill. They cut two willow poles, two cottonwood, two elm, and two walnut poles, and four cedar posts about as long as the height of a man. They worked all day doing this, and took them on the hill. Then they laid them crosswise in a pile with sweet grass underneath and put their father's body on top of the pile. The wonder boy said, "Father, we used to love you but now we are going to burn you up and the smoke will ascend to Tirawa; but, father, you are not dead forever, and some day we will see you again."

Story of the Little Rattlesnake

This story differs from the preceding in that the entire narrative was sung, a typical portion of the melody being transcribed. The story was as follows: In the place where the rattlesnakes lived there was a little rattlesnake who cried because he wanted his rattle to make a noise. He said to his father, "I do not see why I don't rattle. I am just like my brothers and sisters but their rattles rattle while mine does not." His father said, "You are not old enough. When you are as big as your brothers and sisters your rattle will rattle like theirs."

The little snake cried so hard that at last they "made medicine" for him so that his rattle would rattle. Then he wanted to rattle it all the time.

The little snake said to his father, "Tell me how a chief's daughter looks. I want to bite her foot." His father said, "A chief's daughter is very neat in her dress. Those who are not the daughters of chiefs are very careless. You can tell the difference in that way."

The snakes' house was located on a road along which the Pawnee used to travel. The oldest snake said, "Father, my little brother rattles all the time. The Pawnee will hear him and kill us all. Make him stop." But the little snake kept on. He even went beside the road and rattled his rattle very loud.

One day a girl came along the road and the little snake thought she was a chief's daughter. He bit her foot and she turned quickly and crushed his head. The other snakes found him and the brother said, "Father, didn't I tell you that one of us would be killed? There is my little brother with his head smashed." That is the end of the story.

No. 77. The Little Rattlesnake

(Catalogue No. 1077)

Recorded by EFFIE BLAIN

Analysis.—Six renditions of this song were recorded and the time values in all were as indicated in the transcription. The principal progression in the song is F sharp–E, followed by C sharp. Thus the tone material is practically the minor third and fourth, although the fifth occurs in the opening measure. The song begins and ends on the same tone, which is somewhat unusual in Indian songs.

UNCLASSIFIED SONGS

When the Pawnee first saw a horse they were frightened. Some ran away and others said, "I wonder what he is dragging behind him" (referring to his tail). A great crowd of people was looking at the horse. At last someone said, "Why are you afraid of this animal. He is very useful. He can carry you and your packs. You can get on him and he will take you from place to place so that you can kill game." Ever since that time the Pawnee have owned horses, and found that horses could work for them.

No. 78. "You Need Not Fear the Horse"

(Catalogue No. 1079)

Recorded by EFFIE BLAIN

Kīrike	we	rūta	hū	re	kīrike
What	now these	coming	yonder	these	what
we	rūta	arūsa	we	si	rax
now these	coming	horse	now these	it	you
su	rīru	kīrike	we	rūta	
it	afraid	what	now these	coming	

FREE TRANSLATION

What are those that come?
Those yonder, what are those that come?
The horse, you fear it,
What are those that come?

Analysis.—No change of measure length occurs in this song and the count divisions are chiefly quarter and eighth notes. The rhythmic unit is well defined and the six renditions are uniform in every respect. The minor triad and second constitute the tone material, and four-fifths of the intervals are minor thirds.

A man once volunteered to follow a war party and had gone only about halfway to the place of fighting when he met the warriors returning. He was one of the poorest men in all the four bands of the Pawnee. Passing through a deserted camp of his people he saw, by the circles of buffalo skulls, that offerings had been made to

Tirawa. He therefore prayed that Tirawa would help him get a horse so that he could kill some buffalo. His prayer was answered, and he became a very rich man. This is the song in which he offered his prayer.

No. 79. A Poor Man's Prayer

(Catalogue No. 1127)

Recorded by JOHN LUWAK

Voice ♩ = 58
Drum ♩ - 58
Drum-rhythm similar to No. 2

Fine

Analysis.—A compass of two octaves characterizes this song, although only two of its intervals are larger than a major third. The lowest tone was distinctly sung. Two-thirds of the progressions are downward and the rhythmic unit is continued throughout the melody. The rhythm was steadily maintained in the three renditions but there was some variance in the intonation.

Only one song was recorded by Mrs. Good Eagle (pl. 2, *c*), who was hostess at a hand game attended by the writer. In explanation of the song she said, "I was sick and lay with my face toward the east. As I lay there I saw a man with his face whitened with clay, wearing a robe and leggings of buffalo hide. He was walking toward the west and singing this song. When I heard it I knew that I would get well."

Analysis.—The ascending octave at the beginning of this song was given accurately in all the renditions. The octave forms the boundary of the melody except for the lower tone at the close, and C is regarded as the keynote, although the third above that tone does not occur. The sustained tones were the same duration in all the renditions. It is interesting to note that these tones usually contain an uneven number of counts. The same has been noted in prolonged tones occurring in songs of this and other tribes.

No. 80. "Everything Will Be Right"

(Catalogue No. 1161)

Recorded by Mrs. Good Eagle

Voice ♩ : 100
Drum not recorded

FREE TRANSLATION

I was thinking, and I knew that everything would be right.

In explanation of the following song the singer said, "What I am going to tell you is not a dream, for I saw it in broad daylight. A star spoke to me and said, "Look at me; I am the one who takes pity on you and gives you good health. Tonight, when you go home, look toward the west. You will see two bright stars. I am the one to the north. I am the one who helps you. When you sing this song you must think of me." Then the star said, "You are not praying enough but I am helping you. I gave you everything you needed, why do you neglect your prayers?" The singer said that ever since that time he had prayed morning and night.

Analysis.—The first seven measures of this song begin on the same tone, the melody descending a fourth or a third during the measure and returning to the initial tone. The remainder of the song contains only the tones of the major triad. Three different phrases are repeated but can scarcely be considered units of rhythm. The upward and downward progressions are almost equal in number. This is the more interesting as the general trend of the melody is downward.

49716°—29——9

No. 81. "The Message of a Star"

(Catalogue No. 1126)

Recorded by JOHN LUWAK

Voice ♩ = 76
Drum ♩ = 76
Drum-rhythm similar to No. 26

The singer who recorded the next song spent his childhood in Nebraska, before the Pawnee moved to Oklahoma. His mother died when he was 3 years old and he grieved a long time for her. His father sang this song to comfort him and said, "We can do nothing when a person dies; we can only pray. Perhaps some day you will be a man and have children around you." When he grew up his father, who was still living, taught him the song and told him of its early use. He made it into a war dance and it is known as his song.

Analysis.—This is one of the songs in which the Indians "cry as they sing," making the intonation unsteady in a portion of the melody. In this instance the first three and last three measures were sung with good intonation but a *glissando* was used on the descending progressions in the fourth and fifth measures. In some of the renditions this was exaggerated and produced a wailing effect. The song is characterized by a large compass and a descending trend.

No. 82. Song to Comfort a Child's Grief

(Catalogue No. 1105)

Recorded by WICITA BLAIN

Voice ♩ = 66
Drum not recorded

Hē - ru tē-kis hē - ru tē-kis   hē - ru tē-kis   hē -

ru tē-kis hē - ru tē-kis   hē · ru tē-kis   ri -

ku - tsi e   hā re wa-hā-a-a-ke

Ahēru [38]	tēkis	rikūtsi	hā	re
Dear	child	stop crying	yonder	there

wahāke
heavens

FREE TRANSLATION

My dear child, stop crying,
Yonder there, in the expanse of the heavens, is where power dwells.

The next song belonged to the first wife of Roaming Chief, who was a close friend of the singer. She had a little girl who died when about 8 months old. Although she had several other children she grieved for this baby and sang the following song about it. The woman's name was Curuk'siwa.

No. 83. Mother's Song for a Dead Baby

(Catalogue No. 1099)

Recorded by EFFIE BLAIN

Voice ♩ = 72
Drum not recorded

Analysis.—This melody is exceedingly simple in both melody and rhythm. The rhythmic unit occurs three times, followed by a phrase which begins like the rhythmic unit but changes to a descending

---

[38] The first syllable of this word was omitted by the singer.

wail in which the tones transcribed E–D–B are clearly discernible but are connected by a *glissando*. The melody tones are those of the fourth five-toned scale and the repeated portion, as in many Indian songs, begins with the second phrase.

A certain man had a dream and in that dream one of his dead relatives appeared and said, "I have come back into this world. You see me." At the same time he heard and learned the following song. When the man awoke he remembered the song and understood what it meant. He dreamed a second time, and the same dead relative appeared, saying, "Remember when we pass from the old earth we pass to a new earth where we are now." The two songs were recorded and the melodies found to be the same. The words of the first were translated, "I am coming," and the words of the second were, "Yonder, whence I came, our relatives are walking."

No. 84. Song Received from a Dead Relative

(Catalogue No. 1132)

Recorded by JOHN LUWAK

Voice ♩ = 116
Drum ♩ = 116
Drum-rhythm similar to No. 26

Analysis.—The chief interest of this song lies in the two phrases which do not contain the rhythmic unit. The first of these phrases is the more energetic, and both bear a resemblance to the unit. The song has a compass of 10 tones and is based on the fourth 5-toned scale. Progression is by an unusually large variety of intervals but the whole tone is the interval of most frequent occurrence.

The next song belongs to a very old woman named Ciïha'rureës whose father was a chief. The singers at the drum sometimes start this song so that she can dance. It was formerly used in a "dance of the chiefs" in which the daughters of chiefs took part.

No. 85. "Father Gave Me a Pipe"

(Catalogue No. 1092)

Recorded by EFFIE BLAIN

Voice ♩ = 104
Drum not recorded

He	a	he	atĭȧs	tĭ		ku		hāk[39]
Exclamation			father	he		me		pipe
ku	tĭ	ku	hāk	ku	tū		rahe	
gave	he	me	pipe	gave	is		good	

FREE TRANSLATION

Father is good,
He gave me a pipe,
He is good.

Analysis.—A comparison of the three rhythmic units occurring in this song will show that the differences are slight, yet they are sufficient to give variety to the rhythm. The song has a range of an octave and contains only the tones of the minor triad and second. It is harmonic in structure and progresses chiefly by whole tones.

Mr. Murie said that the story concerning the following song was recently told him by John Luwak: A man and his wife had one child, a daughter, who had many admirers. Sirirut Kawi (Pushed Forward) entered the lodge early one morning, after the manner of young men courting a maiden. The man said to his wife, "Did you notice that young man?"

He came again, and then the woman said to her husband, "The young man is handsome, he comes of a good family, he has plenty of horses and his arms are strong so that he would be good to support us." When he came the third time they told him to wait for his answer until the girl's relatives could discuss the matter. So they called their

---

[39] The last letter of this word was elided with the next word by the singer.

relatives together, the mother's relatives being seated on the south and the father's on the north side of the lodge. The father's relatives left the decision with the mother's relatives, who decided that the girl should be allowed to marry the young man. Many presents were distributed. The young man's relatives gave presents, and the young man gave a fine horse to the father and mother of the girl. The next day the old man gave the horse to his wife. There were buffalo robes and many valuable articles among the presents.

All went well for a time, and then the young man began to beat his wife and abuse her. The girl's mother begged her father to interfere, but he refused to do so. She said, "You claim to be a brave man; why do you not make our son-in-law stop beating his wife?"

He said, "Do you remember one beautiful morning when you said the young man was handsome, that he came of good family, had many horses, and his arms were strong?"

"Yes."

"Do you remember that my relatives sat on the north and yours on the south side of the lodge, and that my relatives left the decision to yours?"

"Yes."

"So your people sold our daughter to that man. We have no right to interfere with his property. He gave the ponies. He gave a fine pony to us. Didn't I give you that pony?"

"Yes."

"Get a kettle. Put it on the fire and put water in it." She did so.

"Now take your parflêche bag and put the finest of your dried meat in the pot. When the soup is done you must bring me some in a wooden bowl."

When she brought the soup he told her to sit beside him and eat. As they ate he said, "What nice fat! What fine meat this is! Who got it for you?"

"Our son-in-law."

"You like the meat that our son-in-law brings us? He punishes our daughter for her own good. He does not want her to run around the camp foolishly. He wants her to be a good cook and to look after things in the lodge."

Then the woman stopped finding fault with her son-in-law.

The young man was well liked by the chiefs. They asked him to join their societies and later he became a chief. He and his wife had one child, a boy. This little boy liked to stay with his grandfather, who told him stories. His grandfather was Sarītsaris (Mad Chief), a brave man of the Chaui Band. The little boy cooled his grandfather's mush or soup by swinging the dish back and forth, then he set it before the old man.

When the little boy was about half-grown he heard that a war party was to start. He told his mother that he wanted to go, and he wanted her and his grandmother to make him some moccasins. He also wanted arrows, a bow and a quiver, and all the equipment of a warrior. When the old man heard this he called the boy and said, "Do you realize what you are doing?"

"Yes, I am grown to be a man."

"Do you have dreams at night?"

"Yes."

"Can you relate some of them?"

"Yes."

"Tell one to me."

"In my dream I was with a war party. I found myself coming toward home through deep snow."

"That is enough," said the old man. "You can go."

The women had sent the boy to his grandfather, thinking he would keep him at home, and they were greatly surprised to learn that the grandfather had told the boy to go with the warriors. It was fall when the war party started. As winter was coming near it was noised through the camp that all the war party had been killed and the people began to mourn. The women of this family mourned exceedingly and cut their flesh with knives, but the old man sat and laughed at them, or smoked his pipe. This went on for about 10 days. Then his wife said, "You did not care for our grandchild," and his daughter said, "Why do you not mourn?" The old man said to his wife, "You remember that you turned the boy over to me when he wanted to go to war. You made moccasins for him and filled his quiver with arrows. I questioned him and found that he had had a dream in which he was returning alone through deep snow. That dream will come true. He is coming home, so I want you all to stop mourning."

They would not believe him, but one day, after a snow, some people going out from the village met the young man returning. He said, "All the warriors were killed except myself."

The man rode back and cried through the village, "Sarĭtsaris' grandchild is coming through the deep snow."

Everyone in the lodge was excited, except the old man. He did not rush out to meet his grandson. The women urged him to go, but he said, "He is coming; never mind."

When the young man entered the lodge his grandfather said, "Sit on my knees." The old man passed his hands downward over the young man's head and body in the tribal manner of "blessing," and said, "I believed in your dream and now you are here."

Then he told him to sit yonder and said, "I ask you—when attacked, did you hide in a ravine? When you were a little boy and cooled my mush I told you that I never wanted to hear that your body was found in a ravine. I said that if you must be killed, let it be on a hilltop, fighting in the open. I told you not to run away. Did you fight the enemy? Is it possible that you had gone on an errand and on your return found the fight going on and ran home instead of joining your comrades? I told you always to tell the truth. Don't lie to me now. Tell me the truth."

The young man said, "This will tell the story," and he exposed his arm, which was raw and sore from wrist to elbow, where the bow-string had stung him. The boy said, "I did not even throw away my buffalo robe. I fought until night and then they let me alone."

The old man said, "Now your name shall be Sirirut Kawi, the same as your father's. If you had been killed I would not have shed a tear, for I urged you to go on the warpath."

So the young man lived with his grandfather until the next summer, when the village was attacked by the enemy. The young man went out and was killed. The news was brought into the village and the old man heard it. He took his robe of bear skin, threw it over his shoulder, and went about the camp telling how kind the young man was to the old and sick. Returning home, he said, "You waved the bowl of mush to cool it. I shall miss you."

People said his heart was like a stone until he sang this song. Then he wept. In the first portion of the words he sings about himself and his pride in his grandson, and in the latter portion he sings about the young man.

No. 86. Mad Chief Mourns for His Grandson

(Catalogue No. 1096)

Recored by EFFIE BLAIN

Voice ♩ = 84
Drum not recorded

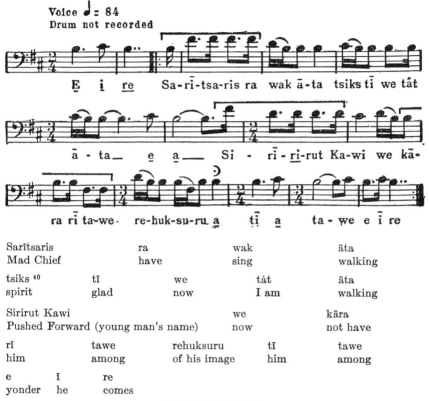

Sarītsaris	ra	wak	āta
Mad Chief	have	sing	walking
tsiks [40]	tī	we	tȧt	āta
spirit	glad	now	I am	walking

Sirirut Kawi	we	kāra
Pushed Forward (young man's name)	now	not have

rī	tawe	rehuksuru	tī	tawe
him	among	of his image	him	among

e	ī	re
yonder	he	comes

FREE TRANSLATION

Mad Chief sings as he walks, his spirit is glad as he walks.
Pushed Forward is no longer among us, yet we seem to see him;
Yonder he comes.

Analysis. This melody lies partly above and partly below the keynote, a melodic form occurring less frequently among the Pawnee than in certain other tribes. The song begins and ends on the same tone and is based on the minor triad and second. It is minor in tonality and almost two-thirds of the intervals are whole tones.

---

[40] The full form of the word is *tsiksu.*

MELODIC ANALYSIS

TABLE 1.—TONALITY

	Serial numbers of songs	Number	Per cent
Major tonality	3, 4, 7, 8,10, 11, 16, 19, 22, 26, 30, 31, 32, 35, 36, 39, 43, 46, 60, 61, 62, 64, 68, 69, 70, 72, 73, 74, 79, 81, 82, 83, 84.	33	38
Minor tonality	2, 6, 9, 12, 13, 14, 15, 17, 18, 20, 21, 23, 24, 25, 27, 33, 34, 37, 38, 44, 45, 48, 50, 51, 52, 54, 55, 56, 57, 58, 59, 63, 65, 66, 67, 76, 77, 78, 85, 86.	39	46
Both major and minor	29 (same keynote)	1	1
Third lacking	1, 5, 28, 40, 41, 42, 47, 49, 53, 71, 80	12	14
Irregular [1]	75	1	1
Total		86	

TABLE 2.—FIRST NOTE OF SONG—ITS RELATION TO KEYNOTE

	Serial numbers of songs	Number	Per cent
Beginning on the—			
Thirteenth	66	1	1
Twelfth	1, 20, 22, 25, 26, 27, 59	7	8
Eleventh	13	1	1
Tenth	4, 6, 11, 17, 19, 23, 24, 31, 60, 61, 63, 68, 82, 84	14	16
Ninth	8, 12, 21, 28	4	5
Octave	2, 3, 7, 10, 30, 32, 34, 35, 36, 37, 62, 69, 71, 72, 78, 79, 81	17	20
Sixth	74	1	1
Fifth	5, 9, 12, 14, 15, 33, 38, 40, 46, 48, 49, 53, 54, 55, 56, 64, 65, 67, 70, 83, 85.	21	24
Fourth	42, 50	2	2
Third	16, 45, 52, 76	4	5
Second	43, 44	2	2
Keynote	29, 39, 41, 47, 51, 57, 58, 73, 77, 80, 86	11	13
Irregular	75	1	1
Total		86	

TABLE 3.—LAST NOTE OF SONG—ITS RELATION TO KEYNOTE

	Serial numbers of songs	Number	Per cent
Ending on the—			
Fifth	5, 6, 9, 16, 28, 33, 43, 45, 48, 50, 52, 58, 65, 66, 67, 70, 73, 80, 83, 84, 85.	21	24
Third	17, 64	2	1
Keynote	1, 2, 3, 4, 7, 8, 10, 11, 12, 13, 14, 15, 18, 19, 20, 21, 22, 23, 24, 25, 26, 27, 29, 30, 31, 32, 34, 35, 36, 37, 38, 39, 40, 41, 42, 44, 46, 47, 49, 51, 53, 54, 55, 56, 57, 59, 60, 61, 62, 63, 68, 69, 71, 72, 74, 76, 77, 78, 79, 81, 82, 86.	62	72
Irregular	75	1	1
Total		86	

[1] A song is thus classified if the tones do not have an apparent relation to a keynote.

TABLE 4.—LAST NOTE OF SONG—ITS RELATION TO COMPASS OF SONG

	Serial numbers of songs	Number	Per cent
Songs in which final tone is—			
Lowest tone in song	1, 4, 5, 6, 8, 10, 11, 13, 14, 15, 18, 19, 20, 21, 22, 25, 26, 27, 28, 29, 30, 31, 32, 34, 35, 36, 37, 39, 40, 42, 43, 44, 45, 48, 49, 50, 51, 53, 54, 55, 57, 58, 59, 60, 61, 62, 63, 64, 65, 66, 67, 68, 69, 70, 71, 72, 73, 75, 76, 77, 78, 79, 80, 81, 82, 83, 84, 85.	68	78
Immediately preceded by—			
Fourth below	3, 7	2	2
Minor third below	41	1	1
Whole tone below	12, 23	2	2
Semitone below	38, 56	2	2
Minor third below, with minor third below in a previous measure.	16	1	1
Minor third below, with fourth below in a previous measure.	47	1	1
Whole tone below, with a whole tone below in a previous measure.	52	1	1
Songs containing—			
An octave below the final tone.	74	1	1
A fourth below the final tone.	2, 46, 86	3	3
A major third below the final tone.	24, 33	2	2
A minor third below the final tone.	17	1	1
A semitone below the final tone.	9	1	1
Total		86	

TABLE 5.—NUMBER OF TONES COMPRISED IN COMPASS OF SONG

	Serial numbers of songs	Number	Per cent
Compass of—			
Seventeen tones	29, 30, 69, 79	4	5
Thirteen tones	6, 26, 64, 66	4	5
Twelve tones	1, 20, 22, 24, 25, 27, 28, 31, 59, 84,	10	11
Eleven tones	2, 3, 7, 11, 13, 23, 67, 80	8	9
Ten tones	4, 16, 17, 18, 33, 60, 61, 63, 68, 70, 78, 82	12	14
Nine tones	5, 8, 9, 10, 21,	5	6
Eight tones	19, 32, 34, 35, 36, 37, 47, 48, 50, 62, 65, 71, 72, 73, 74, 81, 83, 85, 86	19	22
Seven tones	41, 43, 52	3	3
Six tones	12, 38, 44, 45, 49, 56, 75	7	8
Five tones	14, 15, 40, 46, 51, 53, 54, 55, 57, 58, 76, 77	12	14
Four tones	42	1	1
Three tones	39	1	1
Total		86	

TABLE 6.—TONE MATERIAL

	Serial numbers of songs	Number	Per cent
First 5-toned scale	28, 41, 47, 49, 80	5	6
Second 5-toned scale	13, 20, 34, 38, 44, 52, 63	7	8
Fourth 5-toned scale	3, 22, 30, 31, 35, 61, 83, 84	8	9
Major triad	7	1	1
Major triad and sixth	81	1	1
Major triad and fourth	36	1	1
Major triad and second	8, 76	2	2
Minor triad and fourth	14, 58, 59, 77	4	5
Minor triad and second	15, 33, 51, 78, 85, 86,	6	7
Octave complete	4, 23, 25, 37	4	5
Octave complete except seventh.	10, 12, 26, 27, 43, 46, 68, 69	8	9
Octave complete except seventh and sixth.	11, 21, 48, 50, 57, 65, 82	7	8
Octave complete except seventh and fourth.[1]	45	1	1
Octave complete except seventh and second.	9, 16, 32, 62, 67, 72	6	7
Octave complete except sixth.	56, 60	2	2
Octave complete except sixth and fourth.	2, 18, 64, 66	4	5
Octave complete except fourth.	6, 24, 70, 73, 79	5	6
First, third, fourth, and fifth tones.	54, 55	2	2
First, second, fourth, and fifth tones.	1, 53, 71	3	3
First, second, fifth, and sixth tones.	5, 74	2	2
Other combinations of tones	17, 19, 39, 40, 42	5	6
Both major and minor (same keynote).	29	1	1
Irregular	75	1	1
Total		86	

[1] This song is minor in tonality. The fourth and seventh are the omitted scale degrees in the fourth 5-toned scale, but in that scale the third and sixth above the keynote are major intervals, constituting a scale that is major in tonality.

TABLE 7.—ACCIDENTALS

	Serial numbers of songs	Number	Per cent
Songs containing—			
No accidentals	1, 2, 3, 4, 5, 6, 7, 8, 10, 11, 12, 13, 14, 15, 16, 17, 18, 19, 20, 21, 22, 23, 24, 25, 26, 27, 28, 30, 31, 32, 33, 34, 35, 36, 37, 39, 40, 41, 42, 43, 44, 45, 46, 47, 48, 49, 50, 51, 52, 53, 54, 55, 57, 58, 59, 60, 61, 63, 65, 67, 68, 69, 70, 71, 72, 73, 74, 76, 77, 78, 79, 80, 81, 82, 83, 84, 85, 86.	78	92
Seventh raised a semitone.	38, 56, 66	3	3
Fourth raised a semitone.	9, 62	2	2
Second raised a semitone.	64	1	1
Major and minor (same keynote).	29	1	1
Irregular	75	1	1
Total		86	

TABLE 8.—STRUCTURE

	Serial numbers of songs	Number	Per cent
Melodic	1, 4, 5, 8, 9, 10, 11, 13, 14, 17, 18, 19, 21, 24, 25, 26, 28, 29, 31, 35, 37, 38, 40, 41, 42, 43, 44, 45, 46, 47, 49, 50, 53, 54, 58, 60, 66, 67, 68, 69, 70, 71, 73, 74, 77, 80, 83, 84.	48	56
Melodic with harmonic framework.	2, 12, 15, 20, 22, 27, 36, 48, 59, 61, 62, 63, 64, 82, 86	15	18
Harmonic	3, 6, 7, 16, 23, 30, 32, 33, 34, 39, 51, 52, 55, 56, 57, 65, 72, 76, 78, 79, 81, 85.	22	25
Irregular		1	1
Total		86	

TABLE 9.—FIRST PROGRESSION—DOWNWARD AND UPWARD

	Serial numbers of songs	Number	Per cent
Downward	1, 2, 3, 4, 6, 7, 8, 9, 12, 13, 14, 15, 17, 19, 20, 21, 22, 23, 24, 25, 26, 27, 28, 30, 32, 33, 34, 35, 36, 37, 38, 40, 42, 45, 46, 48, 50, 52, 53, 54, 55, 56, 59, 60, 61, 62, 63, 64, 65, 66, 68, 69, 71, 72, 74, 76, 77, 79, 81, 82, 84, 85.	62	71
Upward	5, 10, 11, 16, 18, 29, 31, 39, 41, 43, 44, 47, 49, 51, 57, 58, 67, 70, 73, 75, 78, 80, 83, 86.	24	28
Total		86	

TABLE 10.—TOTAL NUMBER OF PROGRESSIONS—DOWNWARD AND UPWARD

	Number	Per cent
Downward	1,393	64
Upward	786	36
Total	2,179	

TABLE 11.—INTERVALS IN DOWNWARD PROGRESSION

	Number	Per cent
Intervals of an—		
Octave	2	
Seventh	4	
Major sixth	4	
Minor sixth	10	1
Fifth	12	1
Fourth	158	11
Major third	139	10
Minor third	322	24
Major second	635	45
Minor second	107	7
Total	1,393	

TABLE 12.—INTERVALS IN UPWARD PROGRESSION

	Number	Per cent
Intervals of an—		
Eleventh	1	
Tenth	2	
Ninth	2	
Octave	19	*2*
Seventh	2	
Major sixth	16	*2*
Minor sixth	20	*2*
Fifth	65	*8*
Fourth	112	*14*
Major third	74	*9*
Minor third	119	*14*
Major second	286	*37*
Minor second	68	*9*
Total	786	

TABLE 13.—AVERAGE NUMBER OF SEMITONES IN AN INTERVAL

Number of songs	86
Number of intervals	2,179
Number of semitones	6,856
Average number of semitones in an interval	3.18

RHYTHMIC ANALYSIS

TABLE 14.—PART OF MEASURE ON WHICH SONG BEGINS

	Serial numbers of songs	Number	Per cent
Beginning on unaccented part of measure.	1, 3, 8, 9, 11, 16, 20, 23, 25, 28, 32, 34, 36, 37, 41, 42, 43, 46, 47, 48, 51, 55, 58, 59, 60, 61, 62, 63, 64, 65, 66, 67, 70, 75, 76, 77, 78, 82, 83, 84, 85, 86.	42	*50*
Beginning on accented part of measure.	2, 4, 5, 6, 7, 10, 12, 13, 14, 15, 17, 18, 19, 21, 22, 24, 26, 27, 29, 30, 31, 33, 35, 38, 39, 40, 44, 45, 49, 50, 52, 53, 54, 56, 57, 68, 69, 71, 72, 73, 74, 79, 80, 81.	44	*50*
Total		86	

TABLE 15.—RHYTHM (METER) OF FIRST MEASURE

	Serial numbers of songs	Number	Per cent
First measure in—			
2–4 time	5, 6, 8, 9, 10, 11, 12, 14, 15, 18, 19, 20, 22, 23, 24, 25, 29, 30, 31, 32, 35, 36, 37, 39, 40, 42, 43, 44, 45, 46, 49, 50, 52, 53, 54, 55, 57, 58, 60, 61, 62, 65, 67, 68, 71, 72, 73, 74, 75, 76, 80, 81, 82, 86.	54	*63*
3–4 time	1, 2, 3, 4, 7, 13, 17, 21, 27, 28, 33, 34, 38, 41, 47, 48, 51, 56, 59, 63, 64, 66, 69, 78, 79, 83, 84, 85.	28	*32*
5–4 time	16, 26	2	*2*
5–8 time	77	1	*1*
7–8 time	70	1	*1*
Total		86	

TABLE 16.—CHANGE OF TIME (MEASURE-LENGTHS)

	Serial numbers of songs	Number	Per cent
Songs containing no change of time.	1, 9, 32, 34, 41, 46, 49, 50, 54, 60, 62, 63, 64, 67, 69, 71, 72, 75, 76, 78, 84, 85.	22	26
Songs containing a change of time.	2, 3, 4, 5, 6, 7, 8, 10, 11, 12, 13, 14, 15, 16, 17, 18, 19, 20, 21, 22, 23, 24, 25, 26, 27, 28, 29, 30, 31, 33, 35, 36, 37, 38, 39, 40, 42, 43, 44, 45, 47, 48, 51, 52, 53, 55, 56, 57, 58, 59, 61, 65, 66, 68, 70, 73, 74, 77, 79, 80, 81, 82, 83, 86.	64	74
Total		86	

TABLE 17.—RHYTHMIC UNIT OF SONG

	Serial numbers of songs	Number	Per cent
Songs containing—			
No rhythmic unit	2, 3, 16, 17, 23, 27, 29, 30, 31, 38, 74, 77, 81	13	15
One rhythmic unit	4, 5, 6, 7, 9, 10, 11, 13, 14, 15, 18, 19, 25, 32, 36, 41, 45, 46, 49, 50, 54, 60, 61, 62, 63, 64, 67, 69, 70, 71, 73, 75, 76, 78, 79, 80, 82, 83, 84, 86.	40	46
Two rhythmic units	1, 8, 12, 20, 21, 22, 24, 28, 33, 34, 35, 37, 39, 40, 44, 47, 48, 52, 53, 55, 56, 58, 59, 65, 66, 68.	26	30
Three rhythmic units	26, 42, 43, 51, 57, 72, 85	7	8
Total		86	

TABLE 18.—RHYTHM OF DRUM [1]

	Serial numbers of songs	Number	Per cent
Eighth notes uniformly accented.	2, 3, 4, 5, 6, 7, 8, 9, 11, 12, 13, 14, 15, 32, 36, 47, 52, 61, 65, 71, 79	21	24
Quarter notes uniformly accented.	26, 31, 34, 57, 63, 69, 81, 84	8	9
Each beat followed by an unaccented beat corresponding to the second count of a triplet.	48	1	
Drum not recorded	1, 10, 16, 17, 18, 19, 20, 21, 22, 23, 24, 25, 27, 28, 29, 30, 33, 35, 37, 38, 39, 40, 41, 42, 43, 44, 45, 46, 49, 40, 51, 53, 54, 55, 56, 58, 59, 60, 62, 64, 66, 67, 68, 70, 72, 73, 74, 75, 76, 77, 78, 80, 82, 83, 85, 86.	56	65
Total		86	

[1] This table is not carried forward in the cumulative analyses. See p. 17.

AUTHORITIES CITED

CULIN, STEWART. Games of the North American Indians. Twenty-fourth Ann. Rept. Bur. Amer. Ethn., Washington, 1907.

DENSMORE, FRANCES. Chippewa Music. Bur. Amer. Ethn., Bull. 45, Washington, 1910.

———— Chippewa Music—II. Bur. Amer. Ethn., Bull. 53, Washington, 1913.

———— Teton Sioux Music. Bur. Amer. Ethn., Bull. 61, Washington, 1918.

———— Northern Ute Music. Bur. Amer. Ethn., Bull. 75, Washington, 1922.

———— Mandan and Hidatsa Music. Bur. Amer. Ethn., Bull. 80, Washington, 1923.

———— Papago Music. Bur. Amer. Ethn., Bull. 90, Washington, 1929.

DORSEY, GEORGE A. How the Pawnee captured the Cheyenne medicine arrows. Amer. Anthrop., n. s. vol. v, pp. 644–658, Lancaster, Pa., 1903.

———— Traditions of the Skidi Pawnee. Mem. Amer. Folk-Lore Soc., vol. VIII, Boston and New York, 1904.

———— The Pawnee: Mythology (Part I). Carnegie Inst. Publ. no. 59, Washington, 1906.

FLETCHER, ALICE C. The Hako: a Pawnee Ceremony. Twenty-second Ann. Rept. Bur. Amer. Ethn., pt. 2, Washington, 1903.

———— [Article] Pawnee. Bur. Amer. Ethn., Bull. 30, pt. 2, pp. 213–216, Washington, 1910.

———— and LA FLESCHE, FRANCIS. The Omaha Tribe. Twenty-seventh Ann. Rept. Bur. Amer. Ethn., Washington, 1911.

HELMHOLTZ, H. L. F. The sensations of tone as a physiological basis for the theory of music. Translated by A. J. Ellis. 2d ed., London, 1885.

INDIAN AFFAIRS. Laws and Treaties. vol. I (Laws). vol. II (Treaties). Compiled and edited by Charles J. Kappler. Washington, 1904.

———— Report of the Bureau of Indian Affairs for the year ending June 30, 1928. Washington, 1928.

JAMES, EDWIN. Account of an expedition from Pittsburg to the Rocky Mountains under the command of Maj. Stephen H. Long, vol. I, Philadelphia, 1823.

LA FLESCHE, FRANCIS. See Fletcher, Alice C., and La Flesche.

LINTON, RALPH. The Thunder Ceremony of the Pawnee. Field Museum of Natural History, Leaflet No. 5, Chicago, 1922.

———— The Sacrifice to the Morning Star by the Skidi Pawnee. Ibid., No. 6.

———— Annual Ceremony of the Pawnee Medicine Men. Ibid., No. 8, 1923.

LOWIE, ROBERT H. Societies of the Hidatsa and Mandan Indians. Anthrop. Papers Amer. Mus. Nat. Hist., vol. XI, pt. 3, pp. 219–358, New York, 1913.

MOONEY, JAMES. The Ghost-dance Religion and the Sioux Outbreak of 1890. Fourteenth Ann. Rept. Bur. Ethn., pt. 2, Washington, 1897.

INDEX

128   INDEX

066954